Discovering
the L.A. Art World

I0499818

John Marcella Grant

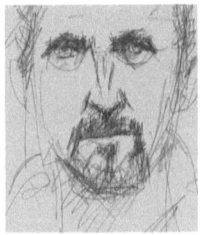

ISBN: 9781694576125

***This book is dedicated to Bradford J. Salamon and Mat Gleason, who inspired me to write this book.

CONTENTS

ACKNOWLEDGMENTS

Thank you to:

Julie, Rachel, Nathan, and Shane Grant, for supporting me as I make art.

Rachel Grant for the cover design.

Shane Grant for the drawing of *Back Seat Dodge '38*.

My parents and Mark and Mimi Grant for your encouragement.

Mosheh Chanan, Ryan Womack, Victor Kreider, Joel Berryhill, Chuck Moreau, Murray Carstens, Len Bierman JD, Phil Moreno, and Cully Lipsey for your encouragement these past years.

Jack Bodden PhD, Aaron Brown, Zach Carstens, John Grant III, Judy Grant, Jeannie Miller, and John Pinkerton, who edited this book.

The artists who welcomed me into their studios.

John Seed for inspiring me with your book *My Art World*.

Joo Young Choi for your intelligent feedback.

David Carrabba for helping me with the title.

Chip Hill for input on self-publishing.

TITLE PAGE IMAGE - Drawing of John Marcella Grant IV by Bradford J. Salamon, Copyright 2017.

(Below, my paintings of the writers John Seed and Michael Lorenzo Porter, who advised me as I wrote this book.)

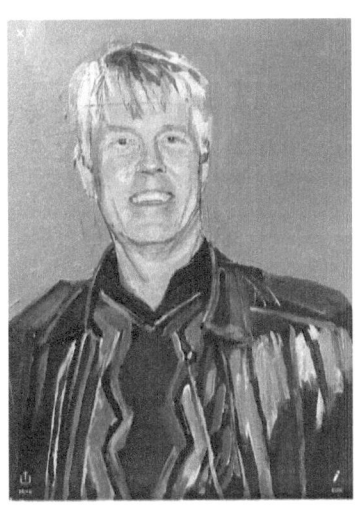

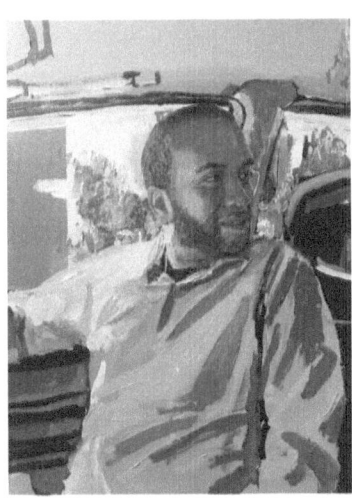

INTRODUCTION

We knock on a studio door in L.A., and an enormous, red-headed man emerges. He looks pissed. "What do you want?" he barks.

"My name is John Grant. Thomas Houseago is my favorite sculptor. We've come from Texas to meet him."

"Thomas does not entertain strangers." He shuts the door in our faces.

––––––

Heraclitus, the Greek philosopher, said, "You cannot step into the same river twice, for other waters are continually flowing." He might be right. But I am hoping in my case, he was wrong. I aim to return to L.A., and once there, thrive in its art world.

The title of this book, *Discovering the L.A. Art World*, describes my aspirational story. In the following pages, I share wisdom received from respected artists in Los Angeles during a series of studio visits. Herein, I describe my efforts to achieve a foothold in the Southern California art scene while still residing in Texas. Optimally, my record will provide inspiration. Mine is not a rags-to-riches story. Many overachievers pen such tales, but their promises ring hollow. They pledge that if one simply follows their program, then they will be guaranteed to reach their same pinnacles of success. In contrast, I have written this book while ensconced in my own ordinariness. The wisdom which follows (from artists like Mark Bradford and Edgar Arceneaux) is practical, and can be implemented where the rubber meets the road. Although my wife and I currently live in Texas, there is for us a wormhole of sorts leading back to California, and it is called "social media." My hope is to return to SoCal as a self-sustaining artist, and social media is helping me to crack open the door (see *my painting, "The Artist," below*).

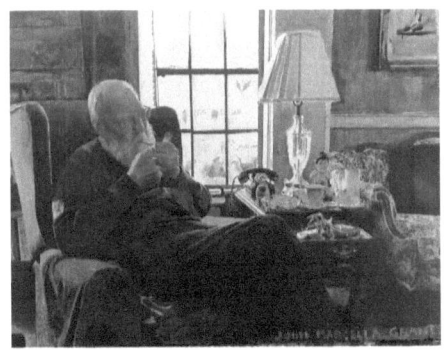

In John Seed's blurb for my book, he writes that I offer "private glimpses of (the L.A. art) world." In his 2019 volume *My Art World*, he describes the "Art World" as a "complicated and foreboding social construct." With that in mind, let's break it down with what I have learned from many firsthand experiences with L.A. art figures. Some of my studio visits were home runs, but others were strikeouts. Before and after our meetings, I visited SoCal museums and galleries as bookends for my day, such as the Los Angeles County Museum of Art (the LACMA), the Museum of Contemporary Art (the MOCA), the Broad, the Orange County Museum of Arts (the OCMA), the Getty, the Hammer, the Norton Simon Museum (the NSM), Blum and Poe, Hauser and Wirth, the Gagosian Gallery (in Beverly Hills), and the Susanne Vielmetter Gallery. It was stimulating to go from viewing masterpieces in museums and galleries to conversing with living masters face to face, all within the same day.

While writing out my memories, I have tried to recall each visit down to its smallest detail. Everything in this book really happened, and writing it has been cathartic. In my attempts to engage with art figures, I wrote emails and made innumerable phone calls. Friends were made on Facebook, often with the use of Facebook Messenger. Free samples of my work were shipped to L.A.

Dozens of studio and gallery visits were conducted. Many art books were read, including artists' biographies. I made connections on social media with the friends of L.A. art luminaries. Countless YouTube art interviews and documentaries were viewed. I shipped my bust of the TV personality Josh Flagg to Beverly Hills to be featured in his show *The Million Dollar Listing, L.A.* (*below, left*).

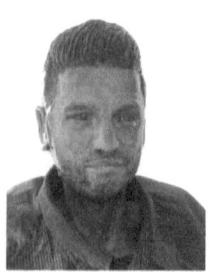 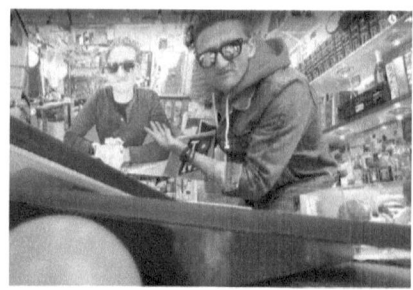

In addition, I convinced the YouTube sensation Casey Neistat to showcase my painting on his vlog (*page 3, right*). On Facebook, I continuously "liked" artists' works. As I made more art, I sent my best images to artists whom I wanted to impress. I fostered mentorships. I identified a mentor of my mentor, and 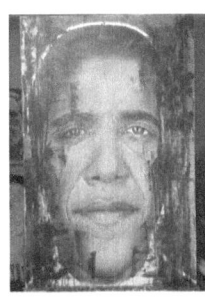 then I made him my own personal advisor. I wrote the actor/artist Jim Carrey requesting a studio visit; I was ignored. I wrote President Obama (*left, in my painting*) through the White House website, and he quoted me in his speech at the Democratic National Convention in Philadelphia. Following this, I again wrote to the White House website, this time suggesting that I might paint President Obama's portrait, and I was denied. I taught art classes, and I traded art for dental work.

I was featured on our local PBS radio station. In addition, a local podcaster named Bailey Mullins interviewed me. I was profiled in our local paper; I was highlighted by a local magazine; I became a Wikipedia arts editor. While I engaged in the above activities, I also completed over sixty paid commissions (paintings, drawings, and sculptures). Furthermore, many prints of my pencil drawings were sold. I took one small step after another in an effort to become a full-time artist, and then possibly moving back to L.A.

As I began visiting SoCal artists, I did not have a preset plan of attack. Rather, as one successful meeting built upon the next, doors flew open. My mindset was to figure it out as I went along. During many interactions, I felt euphoria in my self-discovery, thinking, "This is what I am meant to do! I am wired to be an artist."

Each time I met an artist, I felt like a 1926 baseball fan attending a game at Yankee Stadium. I would "watch the game." Then, I would dine with a Babe Ruth or Lou Gehrig of the L.A. art world.

As the years went by, my mindset evolved. Artists' comments began to resonate with my own studio experiences. I began to understand their moves, especially when they referred to significant artists or important epochs in art history. I went from being a beginner to becoming a practitioner. I learned that the destination in my pilgrimage was not as important as the process itself. This epiphany occurred while I developed as a painter. What I now enjoy most about painting is doing the work, and not obsessing over gaining riches or fame. But honestly, divorcing myself from monetary concerns remains a day-by-day struggle, especially when bills need to be paid.

CHAPTER 1 - THE BEGINNING

In the beginning, my wife Julie and I lived our first thirty-one years in Southern California. Although I grew up in Orange County, many of my formative experiences occurred several miles to the north in Los Angeles County. In 1983, when I was an eleven year old boy, I experienced a brief transcendent experience in the Los Angeles County Museum of Art. Permit me now to paint the picture…

LOS ANGELES, L.A. COUNTY MUSEUM OF ART, 1983

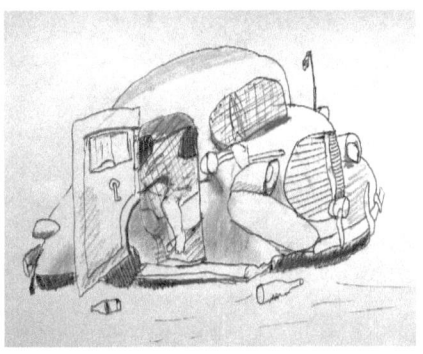

Ed Kienholz' assemblage, *Back Seat Dodge '38* (above), loomed before me. It consisted of a stylized '38

Dodge with an open door revealing two life-sized figures in the back seat; one was made of chickenwire. I was young. "What are those sculptures doing?" I wondered. I had no clue about the lascivious scandal associated with the piece. I thought, "This art is cool. Perhaps they were on a ride and the door accidentally flew open. It's definitely not boring like the paintings in the adjacent halls." I studied the choreography of the duo. This pair of lovers was nearly as interesting as the mammoth tusks which I had viewed at the La Brea Tar Pits next door. I did not yet understand the meaning of the word *composition,* but at that moment, I sure felt it. The wheels in my brain raced. I wasn't thinking about the artist Kienholz; but I did sense a resonance between the two of us. Interestingly, Kienholz and his wife Nancy Reddin Kienholz created many collaborative works from 1972 onward; but *Back Seat Dodge '38* was created in 1964 by Mr. Kienholz alone.

Kienholz, back in his day, was a big, tough, and burly brute. My small body could not have been any more different from his frame, yet I understood his moves - maybe as well as the LACMA curator. Somehow I could intuit why Kienholz arranged the figures in the back seat the way that he did. In fact, I had made similar compositions at home with my Legos. Allow me to explain: There were adjacencies in his work. There was a dominant and a submissive figure. There were solids, and there were transparencies in the chicken-wire figures. I had appropriated these same gestures in my own Lego creations at home. While constructing custom Lego spaceships, I built a mother-ship. Then I made a small battle-cruiser which docked *inside* of the mother-ship's hangar bay. And many of my Lego pieces were translucent.

After a few minutes viewing Back Seat Dodge '38 with me, my parents ambled over to the next large space. They called out to me, "Johnnnnnnn," and I quickly followed. I immediately forgot what I had just experienced with *Back Seat Dodge '38*. I ran to them because I was an obedient boy; I was not transgressive like Kienholz. Even today, my conformity makes it difficult for me to commune with fellow creatives. Often, I feel hamstrung by this incongruity (i.e., being creative, yet also a rule-follower). At that moment in the museum, my mind wandered. Suddenly, I was gripped by a strong yearning for a McDonald's Happy Meal, because in addition to being a conformist, I was also a hungry and observant child. I had noticed a McDonald's on La Cienega on our way to the museum. First things first. I begged my parents to take me there for lunch, and off we went. I believe that my repeated exposure to museums at a young age gave me a strong comfort level with art, and much later, with makers of art.

Five years later, at age sixteen, I worked at my uncle's electrical supply wholesale business at 67th and Main Street called Main Electric, in what was then known as South-Central L.A. I made fast friends with my co-workers, and I happened to be the only Caucasian in the entire warehouse. Once, while I was unloading conduit from a truck, my new buddies came outside to watch. They said I was the first white worker they had seen unloading a truck there since the sixties. Main Electric was not in the best of neighborhoods; one night, my uncle's two guard dogs were stolen. Another time, his rear windshield was shot out while he drove to work. Working in this environment helped me learn how to interact with diverse groups, and this would later help me during my studio visits. Unbeknownst to me, I was working only blocks away from a young

Kehinde Wiley (a prominent artist featured later in this book) while he grew up nearby.

The following year, I found myself doing demolition in the luxurious Beverly Hills home of Veronica De Laurentiis (1950-), the producer of blockbuster films such as *Backdraft*. As my friend and I smashed timbers in her dark attic, I could overhear De Laurentiis' young son bragging to his buddy downstairs that he had hired taxis to ferry him to the nearby movie theater. This was in the days before Uber. He would tell the driver to wait outside for hours to shuttle him back home after each movie. Only in L.A. ... At that time, I missed my chance (by several years) to cross paths with one of my favorite artists, Jean Michel Basquiat (1961-1988). He showed nearby in West Hollywood at the Gagosian Gallery at 510 North Robertson; but that was six years earlier in March of 1983. He was living in Gagosian's beach house in Venice at the time.

Later, as an incoming college freshman at UC Santa Barbara, I drove to school northward from Seal Beach. Kent Twitchell's immense 'Marathon Runners' mural on the sound-wall of the 405 Freeway briefly flashed by me. I could scarcely take in all of it as I raced by at seventy miles per hour in my white Subaru hatchback. "Cool mural," I thought to myself. My understanding was shallow, because in my mind, the artwork was merely decorative and well-painted. Even at this point in time, Twitchell was beginning his tutelage with me; however, I was young and I could only take in a little bit of instruction at a time. I could sense Twitchell's intent, but I couldn't hear his voice. Little did I know that one day we would become friends. How could I be influenced by this man and yet not even know his name? Only years later would I truly be able to appreciate Twitchell's genius. I was completely unaware of the art-flame which one day would roar within me.

At age twenty-one, I became a salesman, selling lights to contractors. All day long, I drove around my territory, East L.A. County. This was my primer, allowing me to etch L.A.'s roadways in my mind. Even now, I can still picture many of them.

A few years later in my twenties, when I was a teacher in Norwalk (a small bedroom community in East L.A. County), I conversed with my principal, Ms. Lopez, about our respective family histories. Boasting about my L.A. street cred, I declared, "My family has been in L.A. for five generations!" She smiled, "That's nothing, John. My family had Spanish land grants dating back more than 200 years." So much for my L.A. street cred.

In terms of personal connections to the contemporary L.A. art world, I brought nothing to the table. My father was a social worker in Norwalk, and my mother was a housewife and a substitute-teacher in Long Beach. Obviously, I was not born with a silver-spoon in my mouth.

In 2003, my wife, our three young children and myself moved from California to Texas (below) in

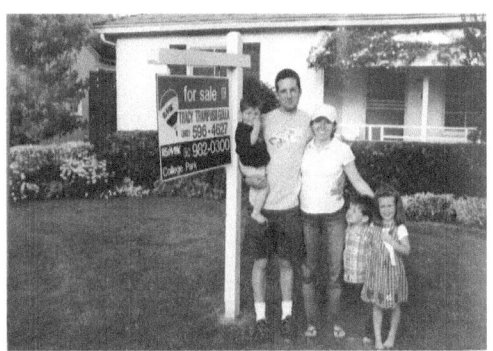

order for me to obtain a master's degree in architecture at Texas A&M, a university which I "discovered" by Googling a strong architecture school in a state with a low cost of living. After graduation, I worked as an architectural intern for three years. My conceptual designs were strong, but I could not recall details, and I struggled with listening comprehension. My employers found me to be likable, but unfit for the job. I worried that I might have had a learning disability, so I had my brain tested with a battery of tests in the Psychology Department at Texas A&M. Everything turned out normal, except for one anomaly — I scored the highest in spatial reasoning of any of their test subjects, ever. Realizing my venture into architecture was not to be, I dove into the arts with a vengeance. Perhaps one day my abilities with spatial reasoning would pay off. Maybe they would lead me back to Los Angeles.(*below, my great-grandmother, the well-known South Pasadena artist of the 1930's-40's, Eugenia Witzleben Grant*)

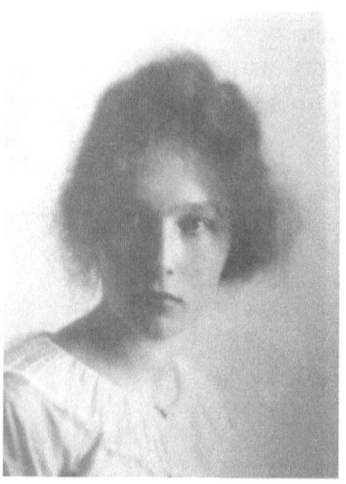

CHAPTER 2 - MARK BRADFORD

~

The door cracks open. A very tall, skinny man smiles down at us. He is six foot eight. He exclaims, "I saw this cute little couple outside of my studio on the security camera, and I wondered, 'What are they doing?'"

"Hi Mark," I say nervously. My voice sounds like Fred Rogers. "My name is John Marcella Grant, and this is my wife Julie. You are my favorite artist, and we came from Texas to see you." (The complete truth was that we were both originally from Southern California, Seal Beach, and San Diego, respectively. But we had relocated to Texas for me to study architecture; we then ran low on funds and became land-locked in Texas.) Mark looks to the right and then to the left, and tries to squash a chortle.

"Well, all right!" he smiles broadly again. "I guess you can come in and we can chat a bit." He leads us inside, and we walk by many tall wooden shelves laden with power tools, extension cords, stacks of colored papers, and small and large tubs of paints and solvents.

Everything is in its place, and the shelves are neatly labeled. We walk into an office space with a few computers. That afternoon, while conversing for two hours, I am gobsmacked by his friendliness. I pull out my handheld portfolio and show him some snapshots of my art. Most of my work up to this point consists of photorealistic, figurative pencil drawings, done technically well, but relatively devoid of any compelling personal content. Unexpectedly, he launches into a litany of encouraging praise.

"These are great! Your technique is amazing! Really John? These aren't photographs? I especially like this drawing here called *Happy Couple*." The artwork shows a man and a woman, each about sixty-three years old. "I love what you are doing here, John! She looks bad-ass, like she just murdered somebody with an axe. It has a very dark feel to it."

Next, he hands me his thick business card. It has a minimal amount of text printed on white card-stock. "Make your cards look just like this." He then zeroes in on my fashion ensemble: a dark green polo shirt, tan baggy shorts, and a pair of flip-flops. "C'mon man!" he exclaims. "There are no flip-flops in the art world! No baggy shorts either! And no collars. You need to buy some black skinny jeans and a tight-fitting black shirt. While I'm thinking about it, make sure not to bring your children to any art events."

Abruptly, he hands me a hard-cover catalogue raisonné of his work. "Here's a gift, John." He writes on the cover page, "Good Luck, Mark, 7-5-12." He leads us down a hallway to his large studio space, where I see a unique in-process painting/collage hanging on each wall segment. As I write this, even now, I seem to recall his main studio was a hexagonal or octagonal space, but I cannot quite remember.

He and Julie chat for a bit, and this allows me a moment to take in my surroundings. His studio is swept clean, with dozens of bright fluorescent light fixtures hanging from a high, dark ceiling. It feels cold in here. Is this what success in the art world feels like? The walls and doorways all around me are oversized, and everything looks like it was designed by a top-tiered architect. In fact, the fit-and-finish of the construction is high-end. This surprises me. I knew that Mark's art sells for crazy prices, but it had not occurred to me that some artists might work in such relative opulence. Off to one side, I observe a small room with a twin bed and a TV. Mark's large studio will one day become home to his non-profit organization *Art + Practice* (conceived and founded together with the philanthropist and collector Eileen Harris Norton and the social activist Allan DiCastro).

As Mark speaks, I get the feeling his work comes about as part of inclusive team effort, a reflection of his outgoing, welcoming spirit. He later confirms this by explicitly referring to his assistants, who help him create his large works. He encourages me to set up a non-profit (a 501(c)(3) organization) related to my own practice (I have yet to follow this piece of advice because I have been busy fulfilling sixty art commissions, helping to raise our three children, and working in my full-time day job as a personal trainer at a local Texas gym).

Mark recalls how he hung out at dance clubs in Europe when he lived there many years ago. These experiences opened his eyes to a much bigger world. I picture him dancing in Amsterdam to the pulsing beat of Daft Punk. "Yeah, John, in Europe, I learned to be very cautious with whom I trusted. The L.A. art world can be tough. Be careful who you let in, and don't be overly trusting." I make a mental note. Having his eyes opened overseas relates to Mark's present-day work: His art looks outward, rather than channeling something from within. Even his materials come to him from an outward focus, as he garrisons a large portion of his supplies by scavenging in the community around him. He purchases the remainder of his materials from Home Depot.

Next, Mark describes how he was "discovered" in 2000 in this very place by Thelma Golden, the prominent museum director and chief curator of The Studio Museum, in Harlem, New York. After graduating from Cal Arts, Mark worked part-time for his mother, doing hair-styling and dye jobs. One day, while he was coloring a client's hair, she was leaning way back as her hair soaked in the sink. At that moment, Ms. Golden walked in. Mark knew this was his big moment, and his life would never be the same. He hollered out, "Thelma Golden! What's up, girl?"

Ms. Golden held up her hands smiling, silently motioning the universal hand signal for "It's OK, Mark, I can wait."

Mark pointed down to his soaking client, and exclaimed, "Oh, her? Don't worry about her! She'll be fine!" Then he bounded over to Ms. Golden, gave her a big hug, and the rest is art history. He had arrived. After recounting this story, Mark smiles down at us and pauses for effect. In the momentary silence, I hear the hum of the air conditioner above. "John and Julie, do you wanna know what the best part was? I bought that hair salon. It became part of this art studio." He points to an area on the floor. "The sink where that woman was soaking was *right there*! And Thelma Golden came in through *that door*!"

Mark shares with us about a 'painting' he made from colored tissues called endpapers. While working in the salon, he would use these endpapers when he gave women perms. Then while making his art, instead of using paints, he appropriated the same endpapers to make giant collages. It was an affordable material with which he could experiment with abandon because of his almost inexhaustible, inexpensive supply. He continues our personal studio tour with a vengeance, proudly showing us his works in progress. He moves from one large painting to another with the grace of a dancer. He stands in front of a single impressive blue piece (about 8x18' in size). My wife Julie jokingly remarks that she would love to take it home with us. He retorts, "You got eighty grand, Julie?"

She giggles, "No way!" Today (in 2019), that piece may be worth up to ten million dollars at auction.

He goes on. "See here? On this one, I embedded lengths of strings here, here, and here!" He speaks clearly, with emphasis. In my opinion, he may be one of the best articulators in the L.A. art world, along with the artist Edgar Arceneaux. "Then, I pull the string like this. See? The string pulls all of these layers of paper backward. Notice the natural crease which it creates? It's like a little valley. And then I apply a clear coat of sealant over all of the papers. It compresses the papers back down. The papers have text on them because they used to be signs on the chain link fences around here. I destroy my art, then I build it back up. I use belt sanders, grinders, drills, and power sprayers to tear down and tear apart. Then I build it back up again by adding more layers of paper. To remove the signs off of fences, me and my assistant, we would both dress in city workers' coveralls. We even had orange cones! We would set up the cones, wearing our matching uniforms, and then we would take the signs off of the fences. One time, when I was overseas, I was trying to bring a bunch of signs back into the U.S. through airport security. The guard looked at my huge pile of signs."

"He said, 'You can't bring that junk through here, man. That's trash!'"

"I said, 'No it's not. It's not trash. It's art.'"

"He said, 'No it's not. That's trash!'"

"Well, anyway, I got it through eventually." Suddenly, Mark focuses in on Julie. "Julie, you are beautiful! And you are great with people! You should have John stay in his studio and do his thing, while you go out, sell his art, and be his manager." Julie smiles at me, beaming; she is enjoying herself. Mark is now officially her new big brother. He lavishes upon her the same overwhelming kindness that I will receive in a subsequent chapter from the artist Bradford J. Salamon. "See what I mean?" he says. "You do have such a pretty smile, Julie!"

A few moments later, I tell Mark that I have been bummed-out lately about my recent career path. As I mentioned before, my family and I had moved to Texas from Long Beach, CA for me to earn my Master of Architecture at Texas A&M (see *one of my drawings, below*).

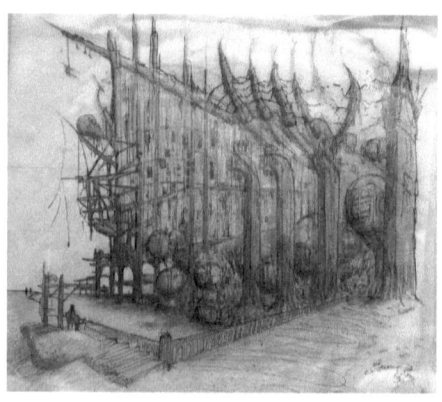

I worked as an entry-level architectural intern for three years; but it was a dead-end. Suddenly Mark becomes very serious, "John. That wasn't your tribe. You just have to find your tribe. You need to man up and get over it! Move on to the next chapter in your life!" So simple. Why had I not thought of this before? Mark smiles down at me like a wise owl. He knows he just fired a torpedo and hit his target dead-on. This feels more like a counseling session than a studio visit.

We converse for another hour. Mark alludes to the fact that most of the L.A. art world is atheistic. Nevertheless, today Mark sure is a blessing to me. We sit in front of his computer with its huge screen and begin to look at many of his artworks and works by other artists. I ask him to click on my website (www.grantartistry.com), and I show him some of the super-extensive art lists which I have made from reading *The Wall Street Journal, The New York Times,* and *The L.A. Times* for many years. There are lists of collectors, lists of dealers, lists of artists, and lists of gallerists, etc. Many of these lists have hundreds of names. He smiles and says "I know many of these collectors personally. But these lists are straight-out weird, John. You should delete these all off of your website right away. You need to look at websites of successful artists, and then pattern yours to look like theirs. And you should just focus your time on making art."

Next, Mark refers again to his studio assistants who assist him with his very large pieces. Upon meeting many other prominent artists, I realize that working with assistants is quite common. I will also discover that artists like Jeff Koons, Kehinde Wiley, Gerhard Richter and even Rembrandt have all employed assistants in their studios.

Mark encourages me to obtain an artist residency. While making my own work, he suggests that I take all of the negatives in my past and appropriate them to fuel my art. He also exhorts me to make an art pilgrimage to Marfa, TX. "You need to go there!" Then he goes on: "You should practice being interviewed about your art in front of a video camera. Also, get your own artist domain for your website and email (for example, studio@grantartistry.com). Look online for scholarships. Don't think so much about other artists. Do your own thing! If you do something controversial, others may not like it. You gotta be ready for that!" Suddenly he becomes more animated: "John, you have courage. You came here. You rang my doorbell. And then you wanted to show your art to me? When you mentioned that you do pencil drawings, I was like, 'Eeesh - I don't know!' But this [He points to my portfolio.] - this is sick! John, what do you want your art to be? Where is it going? Why do you want to do this? What would you tell your sixteen-year-old self if you could talk to him right now?"

I think to myself, "I would probably tell him, 'Don't get your BA in English at UCSB. Don't work for eight years as a teacher. Just go to Cal Arts right away, and then earn your MFA. Start making art right now!'" But I shouldn't second-guess myself, because hindsight is twenty-twenty.

Then Mark comments about how I overshared my hangups and defeats with him at the beginning of our meeting. "Don't be so overly-honest, John. Don't overexpose your heart. Protect your seedling within you like you would protect an innocent child. You are beginning; but believe it or not, you are actually ready right now, man! So be forthcoming. If someone chops you down, press on! Be competitive. Find your kind. When you create a piece in your studio, make four to five iterations of the same artwork. One will inevitably turn out better than the rest. Then continue to develop and refine that one."

He continues: "And your age is good! You are not beginning too late! I started out late myself! You can take some classes if you want. But you do need to follow a few simple rules, especially with regards to your dress and your language." There are a few long pauses, and I can tell it is time for us to leave; so Julie and I say goodbye, and we drive away. I feel stoked; Mark will continue to encourage me in several short emails back and forth over the next upcoming years. I believe my visit with Mark that day fundamentally changed me because he helped me to break free from my chains of self-doubt and defeatism.

Daniel Coyle, author of *The Talent Code*, might describe my meeting with Mark as a "trigger event," a single moment of ignition. Coyle writes that trigger events are about "future belonging… Future belonging activates our built-in motivational triggers, funneling our energy and attention toward a goal" (p. 108). Coyle talks about the idea of "sustained ignition" (p. 126). I believe that I experienced this in all of my studio visits except for one, continually being fired-up during my interactions with all of the art figures. After meeting with Mark, it was like I could hear a quiet voice whispering in my ear, "Hey, this could be you" (p. 132).

CHAPTER 3 - TOBIAS KEENE AND
ROBBI CHONG

~

LOS ANGELES, 2012

Soon after our visit with the artist Mark Bradford, I read an article in *The Wall Street Journal* entitled, "I Love You Man," by Susan Michals about the artist Tobias Keene. It highlights his art and his friendship with the actor Robert Downey Jr. I discover Keene's email address online and set up a studio visit with him and his wife, the actress and model Robbi Chong (daughter of the actor Tommy Chong). Because of our recent successful visit with Mark, I feel emboldened to meet with any artist in L.A. The day of our appointment, Julie and I drive up to a large complex of red brick art studios tucked behind massive industrial warehouses. We find Keene's studio and walk up the wooden steps to a double sliding-glass front door. We knock and Robbi greets us. Resembling her photos on Facebook, she is tall and striking. She ushers us in to meet Tobias, who is seated on an L-shaped couch in his airy, sun-shiny studio. He quietly greets us, smiling, and he guides us on a short tour of his medium-sized space. Tobias and Robbi are both quite friendly. His studio walls are lined with his large paintings which mostly focus on one or two subjects. Each artwork is uncluttered in its composition, and poetic in its stillness. I get the impression that Tobias works slowly and pensively. His measured artistic output greatly contrasts with what I will later see in the studio of the artist Bradford J. Salamon.

In his body of work, Tobias successfully amplifies moments in time; many of his paintings feel like they are depicting memories from his childhood. Tobias is a handsome man, but he looks tired this today, as if he just woke up from a deep sleep. His hair is medium-length and wild. Our visit is cordial, and our conversation feels straight-forward. Robbi fills in Tobias' verbal blanks in a graceful, seamless manner, which reminds me of how Julie is with me. I show Tobias my work, and he studies images of my drawings in my small faux-leather portfolio while he peers through his plastic jeweler's goggles. This inspires me to utilize jeweler's goggles often when I paint and draw in the future. We say farewell, and Julie and I make our exit.

The next day, Julie and I visit the Los Angeles County Museum of Art (LACMA). Amazingly, we come across Tobias there by chance, and we say hello. What are the odds of us crossing paths again in this city of four million, so soon after our visit the previous day? He is with a friend, and neither one of us can think of much to say.

CHAPTER 4 - KEHINDE WILEY

~

I am batting two-for-two in the my L.A. studio visits so far, and I feel indestructable. I have read many online articles about the artist Kehinde Wiley and his impressive body of work. I come across his studio email address online, so I write him, introducing myself and asking if we can set up a studio visit as soon as possible. His assistant promptly writes back. She is polite, but declines my request in the following email: "Thank you for your inquiry and kind words which I will pass along to Kehinde. He now works from Beijing and New York, respectively. Kehinde is no longer in L.A... and regardless, he generally has reservations about hosting studio visits. Thank you again for your email and for sending your wonderful work along. Best of luck with your artistic pursuits."

I don't fault her for writing this. If a stranger wrote me out of the blue asking to visit my inner sanctum, I would hesitate to meet with them. Her polite rejection is my first from an art figure in my series of art studio visits, and I am abruptly brought back down to earth.

As an aside, I recently read in *The New York Times* that Wiley has constructed a beautiful new live/work space in Senegal, where he hosts visiting visual artists and musicians from all over Africa.

CHAPTER 5 - MARK GROTJAHN

~

That same summer, Julie and I find ourselves in a run-down area of Glendale, and we park around the corner from Mark Grotjahn's nondescript studio. The top third of his building's facade is rust-colored brick. The bottom two-thirds consists of barred windows framed by charcoal-colored brick. Grotjahn has not yet moved into his new studio in downtown Los Angeles. I estimate the value of his work inside this dilapidated structure to be in the multiple tens of millions.

Tall palm trees line the street nearby. His studio is armed with massive sets of bars on the windows. The main front door is wide open, but the entry is protected by a heavy-duty, locked, metal screen-door. I hear someone working out of sight in the rear of the dimly lit studio. When I knock, I can see one or two of Grotjahn's box-sculptures inside; they are hybrids of sculptures and paintings. Whoever is working in the back continues clunking, and they ignore my knocks. Earlier today, when Julie and I visited the Blum and Poe Gallery in

Culver City, we saw a few large Grotjahn paintings. They are strong works, and their sales prices are almost beyond belief. We enjoyed their vibrant colors and repeated windmill forms.

Presently, as I stand in front of Grotjahn's studio, I knock a little louder. I can't help but think, "This is one of the most prominent American artists of my generation, and he may be only twenty feet away from me, just out of sight." I am embarrassed to call out his name. I don't want to be *that guy*. Suddenly, I hear a noise from down the sidewalk to my right, about thirty yards away. Out of the corner of my eye, I see a figure motioning for me to come over toward them, and this gives me the willies. I listen to my spidey-sense, and I jog back to our car where Julie is waiting inside. She does not enjoy these art adventures.

"How'd it go?" she asks.

"Dead end."

Seven years later, in 2019, I discover a phone number online for Grotjahn's studio. I dial it, and a female assistant (Or is it his wife?) answers the phone. I recite my spiel; I mention that we will be in L.A. for an art show the following week. I ask if we might stop by for a studio visit. She takes down my name and number, and says that someone will call me back if Mark is interested in meeting with us. They never do.

CHAPTER 6 - PHYLLIS LUTJEANS

~

IRVINE, 2012

It has been a busy summer of art visits for us, and our meeting with Phyllis Lutjeans will be our fifth interaction with a SoCal art figure. Before I proceed with my story, allow me to share my major regret in my art pilgrimage. My wife Julie, our kids, and I were driving south on the 405 Freeway to visit Lutjeans, a paragon of the 80s and 90s Southern California art scene. A few weeks earlier, I had mentioned to my ninety-seven-year-old grandfather on the phone that we were looking forward to seeing him. He and I share the same name, and we were best friends. But with only one day left in Orange County before our return to Texas, I found myself at a fork in the road: (A) keep my appointment with Lutjeans, or (B) cancel the appointment, pay her a $100 cancellation fee, and go see my grandfather.

I rationalized to myself that day that he might not notice because of his lower state of mental clarity, and I chose option (A). To my shame, when I phoned him later for our regular bi-weekly call, he said, "Johnny, why didn't you come see me when you were in California?" I don't remember how I answered. (*Grandpa and myself at another time, below*)

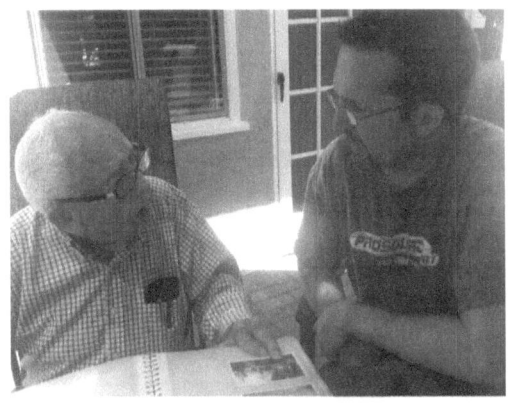

Julie and I unload our kids at Irvine Spectrum Center Mall, and we drive over to Phyllis Lutjeans' condo for our appointment. She is the first and last art figure we will pay for an art consultation. She charges us $100 for today's meeting. We pull up to her modest dwelling in a large condominium complex. It is surprisingly cookie-cutteresque for such a prominent art figure. Ms. Lutjeans is famous for her 1972 interview with the artist Chris Burden. During their conversation, he threatened her at knife-point. She also worked at Newport Harbor Art Museum (now known as the Orange County Museum of the Arts) from 1968 to 1980.

I knock, and Phyllis opens her door, greets us with a smile, and ushers us to a sofa in her living room. I know that this is "holy ground," because we are sitting where many art figures have delivered fantastic art salon lectures. Phyllis is a tiny woman with delicate features and glasses low on her nose. She offers us some water, I hand her a $100 check, and she gets down to business.

Phyllis lectures us for about thirty minutes about art business tidbits, and then she asks if we have any questions. Lately, Julie and I have been beleaguered with stress about money issues related to my pursuit of an art career, and this has impaired our marriage. So we ask Ms. Lutjeans if she might have some marriage advice for us. She smiles knowingly, as if she possesses an ancient mystical secret, clasps her hands together, and exclaims, "Why yes! Do I have a story for you! Many years ago, my husband and I were constantly embattled. I couldn't take him anywhere! He was impossible! He would even hit other men at parties! So one night, I prayed and asked God for divine wisdom about what I should do. Later that evening while I slept, I had a vision; across the wall in my bedroom, in bright white lights I saw the illuminated words, 'Phyllis Lutjeans, you may now extricate yourself from this situation.' So I did! In fact, the very next day, I divorced him!"

Wow! This is NOT the advice which Julie and I expected! Obviously, Phyllis' account does not particularly help us with our predicament. Her second dose of marriage advice is for me to purchase and construct a metal shed in our backyard, and then to convert our garage into an art studio. She admonishes me, "Promptly move your art paraphernalia out of your master bedroom into the garage. No more art studio in the master bedroom." I built the shed and then moved my bulky items into it. But I then realized that our Texas garage is far too hot in the summer to be used as an art studio.

CHAPTER 7 - LAURI FIRSTENBERG

~

After visiting yesterday with Phyllis Lutjeans, a seasoned expert of the SoCal art world, today Julie and I will be interacting with an important young up-and-comer. We park in a side parking lot around the corner from LAXART. We are here to meet with Lauri Firstenberg, the founder, executive director, and curator of L.A.'s nonprofit art space LAXART (founded in 2005). I am amazed that I was able to set up this meeting. We enter, check in, and momentarily wait in the reception area. Several young women zip about the small office; they all appear quite official. I observe that Ms. Firstenberg's staff is made up principally of females.

Suddenly, Ms. Firstenberg strides up to us. She received her Ph.D. in the History of Art and Architecture Department at Harvard University in 2005. In addition, she worked with Thelma Golden at the Whitney Museum (the same Ms. Golden described earlier in the chapter about Mark Bradford). Her fashion sense (as well as the style of the women in her office) is strong.

She is wearing a black serape over a dark dress. Ms. Firstenberg enjoys a quality similar to that enjoyed by Edgar Arceneaux and Mark Bradford: All three speak with alacrity. In fact, her elocution is punctuated with phrases such as 'Zombie Formalism' and 'oeuvres of artists,' which at that time fly over my head. As Julie and I briefly meet with her, I share some examples of my art. She is polite, but our conversation is abbreviated. At the end of our appointment, Ms. Firstenberg looks at me quizzically and asks, "Now John, how did you get this meeting?"

CHAPTER 8 - BRETT RUBBICO

~

Our last visit for this summer of 2012 is with a key Orange County art gallerist. It is about 11:00 AM, and Julie and we pull up to Kean Coffee, a trendy spot in Newport Beach, Orange County (O.C.). We arrive early and wait for Brett Rubbico. He dashes in and takes a seat, looking dapper, with a haircut ahead of its time, short on the sides and business on top. He is cool, with Ray-Ban glasses, and I guess that he is forty years old. As we begin conversing, I am distracted by the words 'Ray-Ban' enscribed in silver cursive on his black frames (Original Wayfarer Classics). He has intense eyes, and focused speech. I observe the businessman/gallerist side of him. He speaks quickly.

Brett begins talking about the L.A./O.C. art world. He is well-connected, and seems on the move. (My feeling proves well-founded, as he and his family eventually leave SoCal in 2015.) He speaks about his gallery (Brett Rubbico Gallery in Newport Beach, founded in 2009, and now transplanted to Colorado

Springs, Colorado). It is a small but important node in the O.C. art world. In fact, the way that Brett describes it, his gallery is like a smaller O.C. version of Mat Gleason's Coagula Curatorial in L.A. — or, more regionally, the neighboring Peter Blake Gallery in Laguna Beach. While Brett's gallery space is important to him, and is rigorously curated, his main focus is on his artists and their work. Brett also mentions that he is friends with and represents the artist Bradford J. Salamon.

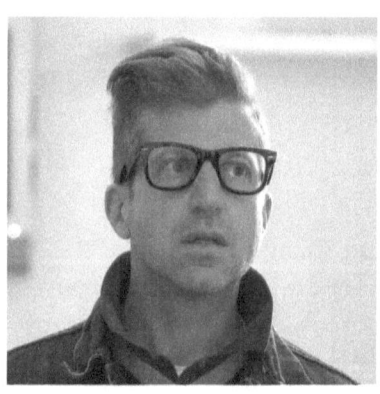

I pick up more from Brett's energy and vibe than I do from his words. He seems skilled with, and aware of, his brand. He wields it. As he leaves, he makes it clear that his time is valuable, and that he would not have met with us unless he thought my work had promise. We part ways, and I watch him hop into his Prius and drive away.

CHAPTER 9 - LADDIE JOHN DILL, CHUCK ARNOLDI, AND RACHEL GRANT

~

VENICE BEACH, 2013

It has been a year since my last series of art visits in SoCal, and now I am back and excited for more. I emailed the artist Laddie John Dill (1943-) weeks earlier, sending him examples of my work (pencil drawings at that time). Today he is expecting me for a short visit. I park a few blocks away from his studio because there are no available spaces nearby, and I walk past a line of trees laden with soiled backpacks filled with transients' possessions. A gym to my right expels muscular men with oversized arms and skinny legs. All about Venice, additionally, I see tall blonde women; innumerable homeless individuals mill about in the mix as well.

I am both excited and nervous as I approach Laddie's chain-linked studio complex. I read about him in Hunter Drohojowska-Philp's *Rebels in Paradise*; I also noticed earlier, on Google, that Laddie was the mentor of my mentor, Mark Bradford, back in the days when Mark was green. Inside the fence is Laddie's studio. Adjacent to his studio is an alleyway filled with transients' tents and rubbish. The trashed alley reeks of urine. It is paradoxical to me that Laddie's beautiful and highly valuable works of art are birthed in close proximity to abject squalor. I walk up to the gate. This is it. I observe an antique intercom surrounded by dusty ivy, and I ring the buzzer. "Hi Laddie. It's me, John Grant."

Laddie answers, but when he speaks through the speaker, he sounds tinny like a cashier at Burger King. "Oh, hey John. Just a sec - I'll come up and open the gate." He seems surprised. Does he remember that I was coming? He walks up to the gate. Laddie looks just like he does on Facebook, jovial and comfortable in his own skin, (much like Jeff Bridges' the Dude, except with a shave). He is of medium height, with a big smile and squinty, kind eyes. Even his walk is relaxed. "C'mon in John. Nice to meet you. Hey man, I like your drawings. They are great! How do you do those?"

I explain in brief, feeling proud of my technique, but privately embarrassed about the lack of content in my work. We walk into his large, open, three-car-garage-sized studio space with a few in-process, galvanized, metal pieces on saw-horses. His two assistants intently grind a large, flat, burnished-metal sculpture. They are skillful and appear not to need direction from Laddie. I introduce myself to them in broken Spanish, and Laddie waves me back toward his private office to the rear of his studio. We walk into his command-center and each take a seat. He leans way back in his swivel-backed chair with his fingers interlocked behind his head. Laddie wears black thick-rimmed glasses, and he looks chill. He waits a long moment for me to speak, and then he breaks the awkward silence.

"So John…Tell me your story. What are you doing here?" I explain that I grew up in Seal Beach, and that my wife, three kids, and I moved to Texas for me to earn my Masters of Architecture from 2003 to 2006. I share how my wife was very sick in the hospital back in 2005 for twenty-eight days. She was forced to relearn how to walk after undergoing four major back surgeries.

"Damn," he mutters empathetically. "That's rough." Laddie is relatable, and I instantly feel at ease. I nod in agreement, and explain that I worked in architecture for three years before discovering that I am more of an artist.

"And now, I am trying to meet the best artists that I can, and learn the ropes from them."

"How did you find me?" he asks. "Why did you want to meet with me in particular?"

"Julie and I met Mark Bradford in his studio about a year ago, and he has been emailing me advice every now and then, and I read that you were Mark's mentor back in the day. So I searched for your website online, called you, set up this meeting, and here I am."

"That's interesting, man. It takes balls to do that. Yeah, I knew Mark decades ago. He was a tall skinny kid, making art, really only making small things. Early on he was just learning, man." Laddie becomes distracted by something on his computer screen. He leans forward, lowers his glasses, and seems to be reading an email. We stop talking. At first I feel uneasy in the awkward stillness, but then (like I did in Mark's studio) I begin to scan his office. It is neatly organized. I know that Laddie has an office assistant because she and I emailed back and forth already. She must be efficient because everything is in its place. Boxes are labeled and jobs are organized on custom-made order-forms. There are compartments for various correspondences. I see that Laddie is not just an accomplished artist - he is a competent administrator as well.

Laddie dishes out a dose of advice for me: "John, I think you should just keep doing what you're doing. Keep making the work. Continue meeting with artists. When you return to Texas, try to meet with artists there who know their stuff. And remember, your path to becoming a full-time artist may take much longer than you'd like to imagine. But that's OK."

VENICE BEACH, 2015

Two years later, I am sitting again in Laddie John Dill's small office. We pick up right where we left off. "Yeah, John. Today we're going to lunch with [the well-known artist] Chuck Arnoldi [1946-]. You'll like him. After that, we'll go check out his studio."

Laddie and I walk together to a nearby restaurant called Plant Food and Wine, and we sit at a small table in the outdoor patio. My new black skinny-jeans feel uncomfortable. As we wait for Chuck, Laddie reminisces how he and Chuck used to hang out with the actor/photographer Dennis Hopper, the architect Frank Gehry, and other artists in Venice in what was known as *The Cool School*. The way that he tells it, they were a macho group of guys.

The restaurant's patio is surrounded by large olive trees and a wall of ivy. I order a hot chocolate with whipped cream. A moment later, I think to myself, "Why didn't I order a beer?" And then, Arnoldi arrives. He really is cool. He would most definitely fit in with any group known as *The Cool School.* He carries himself with a quiet, confident air, and his swagger reminds me of the astronauts in the movie *The Right Stuff*. Even though he is about seventy, he is muscular and built like an olympic diver. He has short spiky white hair, tan skin, and he wears thin-rimmed glasses.

I sip my hot chocolate and eat my sandwich. Right away, I sense that I'm not making the best impression on Arnoldi. After lunch, we make the short walk over to Arnoldi's large studio. Except for Mark Bradford's space, his is the fanciest studio that I will visit in L.A. We walk through his front entryway into a small ante-room. It is cluttered with various paintings on canvas. Up to the left are large canvases 'painted' with dozens of branches instead of strokes of paint.

Then Arnoldi leads us from one large space to the next. The progression of these spaces feels similar to the rooms in the Blum and Poe Gallery: The walls are bare and white, the ceilings are high, and each space is quite expansive. Arnoldi's studio is *very* different from Dill's space. Arnoldi's is posh, almost luxurious; I notice a super-abundance of tubes of Gamblin paints and solvents lined up in orderly rows on tables and carts. I also see pairs of blue gloves, paper towels, and metal cans filled with many brushes. Nearby is an orange can of grapefruit-flavored La Croix, masking tape, and a metal tube-wringer. There are several large in-process paintings on the walls which Arnoldi is painting simultaneously. Outside, through a humungous open door, I see a brand new Mini Cooper automobile. Arnoldi's paintings depict colored squares and various polygons connected by thick diagonals.

I make a few comments about how these works seem to all be about dominance. I point out which shape I think "rules the roost" in each painting. Arnoldi flashes me a classic Mr. Spock expression, raising one eyebrow, while tilting his head to one side. "Ye-esss?" he says. "That's exactly what they are about." I may have hit a single, and maybe I'm on base. Nevertheless, I can tell that I am still very much outside of Arnoldi's personal "circle of trust."

My momentary victory passes all too quickly. Checking out Arnoldi's paintings, I get the sense that he spends as much time thinking about his work as he does making each one (like Mark Rothko did in his practice). There is more than meets the eye in Arnoldi's geometric works. Curiously, I connect deeply with *the work of Arnoldi;* yet I resonate more with *the person of Dill.* Off to my right is a dining table with six black chairs. This room in particular is large, with an abundance of natural light streaming in through the grand glass patio doors behind Arnoldi's work space. The last massive room which he takes us to is where his daughter Natalie works. Her representational paintings are different from Arnoldi's, except for their over-sized scale.

As an aside, the Arnoldis' artistic father-daughter relationship inspires me to reflect on my connection with my own twenty-one-year-old daughter Rachel, who is currently studying graphic design at Texas A&M. She creates art rapidly on her computer, and her sense of composition is beautiful and elegant. Her work is filled with light, grace, and nature's most pleasing colors. In contrast, I work at a glacial pace in traditional media, and I am compositionally cloddish. I look forward to the day when Rachel and I can connect in art dialogue. I think, so far, most of our art bonding occurred when I brought Rachel and her younger brothers to visit many museums when they were little (just like my parents did with me).

(My pencil drawing of Rachel by the Seal Beach Pier, below.)

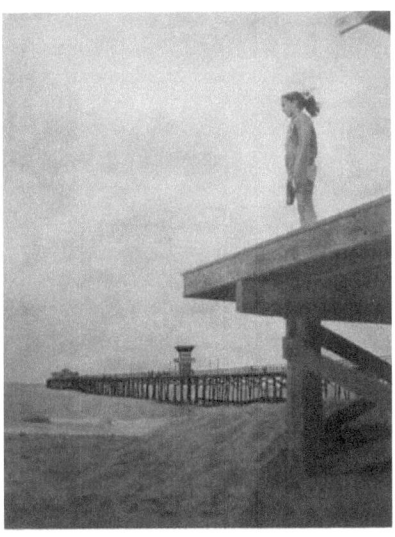

My afternoon with Laddie ends with my hopes temporarily dashed. While we converse, Laddie becomes animated, and he conveys me across town to the gallery complex called Bergamot Station to meet with the well-known gallerist Rosamund Felson. When I arrive at her studio, she makes me wait for an hour; then, when I finally enter her office, she stares down at my drawings for a second before glaring back up at me. She snaps, "I have no idea why Laddie sent you here. I would *never* show anything like this." Her notorious pitbull is nowhere to be seen, and I make a quick exit.

CHAPTER 10 - THOMAS HOUSEAGO

~

LOS ANGELES, 2013

The next day, Julie and I drive over to the impressive studio of the sculptor Thomas Houseago. He is my favorite sculptor, and I love his work. He looks like Van Gogh with muscles, and he is a powerful speaker. But thus far, he is *not* the most accessible artist in L.A. I found his work address online, but could not find his email address. His facility is immense, in a dangerous neighborhood near the 5 Freeway and the L.A. River. In fact, in one of his YouTube videos, he mentions that there was a dead body left unattended in a street nearby.

As we walk up to his studio, three short and stocky assistants covered in plaster walk quickly past us through a gate onto the street. I stand on my tip-toes to see over a fence surrounding the outdoor work space next to his studio, and I observe a large white plaster sculpture. I feel like a kid at Disneyland trying to see a new attraction. We go to Houseago's imposing studio door where I knock, and an enormous, red-headed man opens. He looks pissed. "What do you want?" he bellows.

"My name is John Grant. Thomas Houseago is my favorite sculptor. We have come all the way from Texas to meet him."

"Thomas does not entertain strangers." He shuts the door abruptly in our faces.

CHAPTER 11 - MARK DUTCHER

~

A year later, I drive alone to the studio of the artist Mark Dutcher. I think I am a little lost, even with guidance from my GPS, and I am driving by many Metro train tracks. Ten minutes later, I am inside of Mark's studio; he stands before me. He has a square jaw and kind eyes. His hospitality during my studio visit is genuine. So many artists who I meet are generous, and there is nothing in it for them. This quality continually astonishes me, and Mark is no different.

His studio is exactly what I would want someday for myself: decently sized, messy, and an outflow of a creative mind. Though the busy street outside feels dangerous and menacing, his warm, welcoming spirit and intelligent articulation create an inviting work space. For some unknown reason, it reminds me of the refreshing inn where the sojourner in *Pilgrim's Progress* is rejuvenated. High white walls enclose the room. Tons of detritus litters the floor, and paints, brushes, and remnants of innumerable experiments are everywhere.

As I glance around, it is evident that Mark takes many chances in his work — he doesn't play it safe. Presently, he is flipping through my small portfolio. From time to time, he verbalizes, "Oh, I like that one." He patiently and methodically examines all fifty images. When he is finished, he gives me a half-smile and says, "John, you may want to cull your portfolio down to your ten best works..." Duly noted.

CHAPTER 12 - J. MICHAEL WALKER

~

LOS ANGELES, 2014

A day later, Julie, our kids, and I drive together to visit the well-known L.A. artist J. Michael Walker. On his Facebook page, he describes himself as a "hopeless romantic and perennially emerging artist." We park near his house and knock on his door several times. We are not too far from Dodger Stadium, in a hilly working-class neighborhood with older, small bungalows. Many of the homes have assortments of potted plants in their front yards, including succulents and vegetables, and Walker's front yard is no exception. It is sheltered by a humongous, purple jacaranda tree. There is no sign of Mr. Walker. Where can he be?

After several minutes, he appears out of nowhere. He is a slender man, with long grayish hair and deep-set eyes. We shake hands, and he motions for us to follow him along the side of his house. As he silently glides along, he plucks leaves from his potted herbs, crushes them between his thumb and forefinger, and passes them to our three children to smell.

He guides us back to his dark studio space at the rear of his house. It is small, so we all squeeze in. He begins to casually chat with us. He encourages me to not strive as an artist, and to not try to be famous, but to just do the work. He shows us his paintings, drawings, and a small sampling of his photographic work. He describes how his art is linked with nature, and includes his friends and family, who he cares for intensely.

As he speaks, I'm not grasping the full underlying meaning of his words. He pauses because he picks up on this, and he peers into my eyes to assess my comprehension. It feels like he's reading my mind. He's not just an artist; I can see that he's a teacher as well. Suddenly, he becomes very serious and says, "John, use your time as an artist to devote to your family. If your child needs something at school, drop what you are doing, and go and take it to them. Do laundry. Do dishes. Use your vocation as an artist as an opportunity to serve your wife and children." Later on, I realize that his work is an outflow of his core values.

In addition, many of his artworks which he shows us deal with his wife's culture, and others are spiritual as well. Much of his photographic work is focused on images of women who are his friends. Mr. Walker is an outward-centered artist, similar to Bradford J. Salamon. His depictions elevate and praise individuals in his circle of daily life. As we converse, he suggests that I make two websites: one for my fine art, and another for my commercial work (including my prints of pencil drawings). In addition to being an accomplished artist, Mr. Walker is also a writer, and his many shelves burst at the seams with art books. We run out of things to talk about, so we end our conversation and say our goodbyes.

As Julie, our kids and I walk back toward our car, I reflect on today's visit. I can tell that Mr. Walker believes I am only just beginning my art path. How dare he? Years later, I will realize he was quite perceptive.

Soon after our meeting he writes me the following art wisdom: "Technique will never trump content. There were a zillion technically masterful artists all over Europe in the late 19th century who could paint the most marvelous details; and they're imminently forgettable next to Cezanne, or Degas, or Van Gogh. And all the illustrations in the late 19th and early 20th Century periodicals were rendered by highly skilled engravers, with abilities we'll never possess; they even engraved, and continue to engrave, our currency and stamps. You can sometimes find their engravings for sale. Who wants them? Skill must be in the service of something."

CHAPTER 13 - TAMAR HALPERN AND LLYN FOULKES,

~

LOS ANGELES, 2015

One year later, I am excited to have lunch (described later) with the director and writer Tamar Halpern. Tamar holds an M.F.A. from the University of Southern California's School of Cinematic Arts. She may be best known in the L.A. art world for her documentary *Llyn Foulkes, One Man Band*. In this masterful work, she films the artist Llyn Foulkes (1934-) during many recent years of his L.A. art career. Though Foulkes and I have never met, he plays a pivotal role in this book because of our written interactions with one another.

Decades ago, Foulkes followed the typical American dream. He married, had children, and worked as an artist. In 1957, he began art school. Then, in 1959, he dropped out and began to show his art at the Ferus Gallery. A while later, he was excluded from this venue because of a dispute with the artist Robert Irwin. Subsequently, Foulkes' marriage began to deteriorate. In Halpern's documentary, Foulkes says, "My marriage

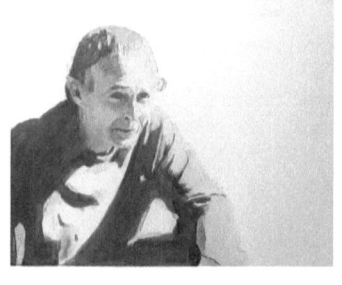 was falling apart, and I was trying to solve it in my painting." Then he worked for years at a frenzied pace on a massive work called "The Awakening" (1994-2012). But his Herculean efforts were all to no avail. Happily, in the last part of the movie (after Foulkes' big solo show), he regained his groove, began smiling again, and appeared more relaxed. *(Foulkes in my painting, left)*

Halpern's greatest success in her film is that she almost completely disappears. When watching, the viewer forgets that there is a director and a camera-person behind the camera, and becomes a veritable fly on the wall. There are no dramatic voice-overs nor commentaries judging Foulkes' successes and failures. Rather, Halpern lets the story play out because she directs with a loose touch.

It is amazing that with the advent of social media, one can watch a documentary, and then in some cases, begin a one-on-one dialogue with both the director and the protagonist about piquant art topics. I begin my back-and-forth dialogue with Foulkes by writing him on

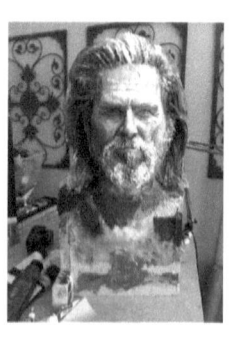 Facebook to share my recent sculptures: "I have been sculpting Jeff Bridges' face *(left)* as a mask over a smaller sculpture of my own face because Bridges is my cool super-ego."

Foulkes responds, "Be careful. My cool super-ego has been giving me lot of trouble lately…"

Just as Foulkes dealt with his

personal struggles in his painting "The Awakening," my series of sculptures are heartfelt as well. As a child, I was small for my age, and bullied from time to time. I grew up in a small beachside community with many older boys, and they often called me demeaning names like

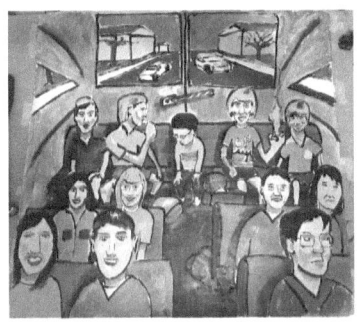 "nerd," "wimp," and "egg-head." One afternoon when I was twelve, I was trying to escape from one boy's house because he and his big brother were beating me up. They repeatedly body-slammed me by jumping off of their couch until they broke my arm (*left, my painting of me and the bullies, in the back of our bus*).

In recent years, in order to retroactively deal with this bullying, I constructed masks on busts which symbolize the strength that I wish I had back then to defend myself. My eight busts are patterned after Jeff Bridges' face, but they are not busts *of* him. They are oversized (at 110% scale), and are built up like geologic layers on top of smaller individual sculptures of my own head. I chose Bridges' face because it is strong. He has an imposing brow ridge, piercing eyes, a rugged jaw, and a Roman nose. In Foulkes' painting "The Awakening," he was vicariously trying to save his marriage. In my sculptures, I was vicariously trying to protect myself *ex post facto*.

While working on my busts, I was working out on a limb, alone, but it was satisfying. I was healing old wounds in the quiet of my studio. Did Foulkes ever feel the same way, like he was working alone? I wonder about this, because my busts have not resonated with many people. I write to Foulkes, "Did you ever paint a piece which you liked a lot, but nobody else really liked?"

He responds, "Yes, John. But it took me a long time to realize that everyone is different." This simple kernel of wisdom may be the anchor to my quest for fellowship in this book. When I make my art, I need to allow myself to 'be different,' and not to depend upon the affirmation of others in my work.

I then ask Foulkes a follow-up question: "I'm curious. What was it like for you being filmed for Tamar's "One Man Band" documentary? Did the camera fade away, and then after a while you didn't even think about it being there?"

He replies, "Yes, I actually did ignore the camera many times, and I would go on a tirade about being left out [of the art world] which I was sorry about afterwards. It took me a while to accept myself in the film after that." Here, I can identify with Foulkes' drive to achieve success and renown as an artist, not wanting to be left out. A number of his fellow artists in the L.A. art world from the 1960s have since skyrocketed to financial success and critical acclaim. Many of the remainder are deceased. In his comment to me, Foulkes is touching on the salient theme of self-acceptance.

In Halpern's documentary, Foulkes displays a direct manner of speech and is dismissive of some of society's norms. I wonder if these same qualities in myself may hold me back as I progress in my art path. Later on, I write Foulkes again, "[Were you angry about being] left out of the upper echelons of the L.A. art world? The main theme which struck me in your movie is that you continued pressing farther and farther in your work into uncharted territory. Then when you got to where you were going, you found it to be a lonely place, and hardly anybody could relate to where you found yourself…"

He responds, "[I was] not concerned so much about the L.A. art world, as just being known as a great artist. I suppose that's what we all want to be recognized for . . . our achievements." When reflecting on Foulkes' unusual process, sensitive temperament, and non-linear creativity, I think he may be a centerpiece for this book, especially in how he relates to my quest to establish community. (Remember what Mark Bradford explained to me years before? "John - That wasn't your tribe. You just have to find your tribe.") It is interesting that out of all of the artists in this book, even though Foulkes and I have never met, he may be the one who I most resemble: His thought-processes are tangential, and his dialogue is highly literal. These traits describe me perfectly. In addition, we both employ an indefatigable tenacity to go after artistic solutions, and we are each loners in our work.

Foulkes and I are also both *non-linear,* meaning the process of our art practice is not sequential. He often thinks and speaks in fits and starts. Foulkes' process in his work is to "make and destroy, and then make again," just like Mark Bradford. On the other hand, though I identify moreso with the artist Kent Twitchell's *weltanschauung*, his artistic method is foreign to me. Twitchell employs science, color theory, planning, along with metaphor, poetics, and multiple layers of meaning. I find meaning in my art *after* my work is complete. I do not fancy coming up with a central idea and then building up a work around this preset theme, the standard academic process for crafting an essay.

Foulkes may disagree at this point with the above comparisons between him and me. He writes me, "Of course no two people are the same just like in the animal world!" Here, he argues that no one is really identical, especially in the makeup of their minds. After reading his above comment about the animal world, I realize that pairing Foulkes with myself is presumptive on my part. I am superimposing myself with a veritable Michael Jordan of the L.A. art world.

I follow up again with Foulkes to gain more insight into his thinking processes when he creates his art: "When you do art, are your thought-processes tangential? Or do you come up with a theme and work around it?"

He responds, "Doesn't matter. Works both ways!" He does not want to be pinned down. No rules. To sum it up, Foulkes writes, "I am [just] trying to create space in a painting. I am trying to do something that has never been done before."

DOWNTOWN LOS ANGELES, MUSEUM OF CONTEMPORARY ART (MOCA) - JUNE 18, 2015

Today we are scheduled to meet with Tamar Halpern at the Lemonade Restaurant, downstairs from the main entrance to the MOCA in downtown L.A. Because of carpooling issues (five of us need to be at different destinations with only one car), Julie and I have our three teenage children in tow (violating one of Mark Bradford's exhortations - "No kids at art meetings!"). We arrive early and wait for Tamar. From our back and forth emails, I erroneously hope she may be considering me as a candidate for her next art documentary. (She had written, "Your work is show-stopping [and] truly spectacular. Tell me about yourself.")

But my wife Julie reminds me that I often mistakenly blow things out of proportion and invent unfounded movies in my brain. In this case, Julie is correct. I notice Tamar just as she turns the corner on the outdoor MOCA staircase. She has shoulder-length brown hair and a pretty smile. We shake hands, she purchases her lunch, and then she joins us at our table. (I should have paid for her meal; but I did not think about this until later.) I eat my fish fillet and drink my lemonade. I notice that Tamar carries herself with the same confidence and poise which I saw years earlier in Lauri Firstenberg. Not too far into our conversation, I realize that my audition with Tamar was most-likely a non-existent aspiration on my part.

After we shoot the breeze for a bit, Tamar remarks, "John, you have your own style that's uniquely yours. Don't shy away from it. And don't worry about art shows, etc. . . . A true artists makes art regardless of the fanfare. That's what I learned from watching Llyn while filming him all those years." We finish our meal together, and we go our separate ways.

A few years later, I watch Tamar's *Llyn Foulkes: One Man Band* documentary time and again. (In fact, I viewed it again today.) While watching, I think I understand why I am not the star of my own art documentary — Mr. Foulkes is telegenic, zany, mega-creative, and charismatic. In contrast, I am calm and mild-mannered. Years later, I am curious about Llyn's process in his work. I write him, "Do you work in silence or with music playing when you paint?"

He answers, "I always paint in silence. If music is played I want to participate!"

CHAPTER 14 - EDGAR ARCENEAUX

~

LOS ANGELES, USC, ROSKI SCHOOL OF ART AND
DESIGN, 2016

Another year has whizzed by, and today I am thrilled to
meet the artist Edgar Arceneaux for the first time at the
Roski School of Art and Design at USC, where he is a
professor. His hiring may have been part of an effort by
USC administrators to resurrect their art program after
its MFA program enrollment shrunk at an alarming rate
in 2016 (according to *The Daily Beast*). The higher-ups
needed to find a few super-stars who could work a
miracle or two.

Edgar began his studies at Art Center College of
Design in 1994. He wanted to share what he was
learning with folks in South L.A. who lacked access to
his newly acquired knowledge from "on top of the hill."
His vision crystallized when he met George Evans, an
artist who created a program called "The Art on
Saturday Program." Edgar and Mr. Evans worked
together for three-and-a-half years. Later, he would meet
the artists Charles Gaines (1944-), Rick Lowe (1961-),

Eugenia P. Butler (1947-2008), and John Outterbridge (1933-), all involved with neighborhood transformation and engagement with communities.

I wait for Edgar in the Roski lounge for twenty minutes. We meet and chat for a little bit, and I give him one of my favorite books (*I Say Me for a Parable: The Oral Autobiography of Mance Lipscomb, Texas Bluesman*). Next, we walk about a quarter mile to the Northern Cafe, a Chinese restaurant near USC. Edgar is tall, and his voice is deep. This quality has the similar effect of a British accent, making him sound authoritative. Later on, I read that we are the same age, but I supposed that he was a few years older..

I prepared for our meeting by visiting the Susan Vielmetter Art Projects Gallery in Culver City twice. During my second visit, I asked the gallerist if I could view more pieces by Edgar. (There was only one of his pieces hanging on display, a large charcoal drawing.) She escorted me to the rear of the gallery to a large flat file cabinet, where she pulled out several of his other pieces. I discovered that the spectrum of Edgar's work is impressive - it includes drawings, sculptures, assemblages, paintings, and now even dramatic productions (very successful ones). One recent write-up in *The L.A. Times* called Edgar a "force of nature," in reference to one of his newly staged plays.

As we begin our lunch together, Edgar transitions into full-on teaching mode. I can tell that he is not only a professor, but also a master instructor. While we converse, he begins with a strong point. Then he supports it with one or two supporting evidences, often with an analogy, a story, or a personal anecdote to make it interesting. Later on, when Julie and I meet with the artist Luis Serrano, he speaks in a similar fashion. J. Michael Walker is also a strong teacher, but he communicates mysteriously, and it takes me a while to unpack his meanings. Laddie John Dill has less frequent teachable moments, but when they occur, one has to be both alert and receptive.

Edgar encourages me to look into the "Thousand True Fans Theory," put forth by Kevin Kelly. Kelly's idea is that artists can sustain themselves (and not have to work a day job) if they enjoy one thousand true fans who buy an average of $100 worth of artwork from them each year. In my mind, the utility of this theory is questionable.

I share with Edgar about my latest series of Jeff Bridges-inspired clay and wooden busts. They each weigh about forty-five pounds, and are made out of wood, unfired clay, and a polyurethane painted shell covered with acrylic paint. I paint on their faces as if the busts are actual canvases. Edgar suggests that I incorporate four guidelines (not hard-and-fast rules) for communication in my artwork, especially with regards to my sculptures:

1. Show the steps
2. Label each step.
3. Write about each step.
4. Photograph each step.

We discuss how a prominent artist in this book suggested to me that the L.A. art world is mostly atheistic, and that I need to steer clear of incorporating God into my work. Edgar shakes his head in disagreement. "No man. I don't agree with that. It is OK to break the rules. Your art can be personal, but it should be related to a larger discourse. The discourse is just as important as the object itself. Your goal, John, should be to create *new ideas*. There is always a mystery hiding behind another mystery." Next, Edgar explains about the four main steps in art:

1. Who are you?
2. What are you doing?
3. Why are you doing it?
4. Why should we care?

He pauses and I complement him on his intelligent articulation: "Edgar, you are one of the better speakers I've interacted with during my studio visits."

"Thanks, man. If you want, you may think about taking a few Toastmasters classes." As our conversation progresses, I coadunate Edgar's art with the work of Mark Bradford, Rick Lowe, and Theaster Gates.

"Don't lump us together," he says seriously. "Our practices are very different from one another." I feel chastised, but I can tell that Edgar has moved on because he is not easily offended.

———

ABOUT TWELVE MILES EAST OF LOS ANGELES, 2017

I pull up to Edgar's house for a second visit, exactly one year after our first interaction. This time, I arrive with a $40 bottle of red wine from Ralph's grocery store. I knock on his front door and no one answers. But I won't give up easily, because I only have one week of vacation during my entire summer and we came here all the way from Texas. So, I walk down his side driveway and call out his name. Then I walk back to the front door, and knock again. Finally, after a few minutes, Edgar steps out, and he looks bushed.

"Hey John. What's up?" His voice sounds hoarse.

"Hi Edgar. I'm here for our eleven o'clock appointment."

"Oh damn. I'm sorry. We just got in super-late last night after a week vacation in Hawaii with my entire family. It was legit." Edgar and I walk around to his back driveway. He guides me on a quick tour of his studio inside of two or three garages, along with some ancillary rooms. He shows me a new involved project that he is working on which consists of books encrusted in crystals and wax. The volumes look like they are encased in stalagmites; and he will later display them in glass cases. Next, I see a few of his works with etched text on mirrors. We chat on a picnic bench for a while, and I sheepishly think to myself, "I should have let him sleep." We part ways. (*my pencil drawing, self-portrait, and my painting of Edgar Arceneaux, below*)

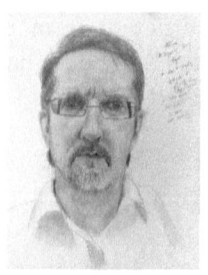

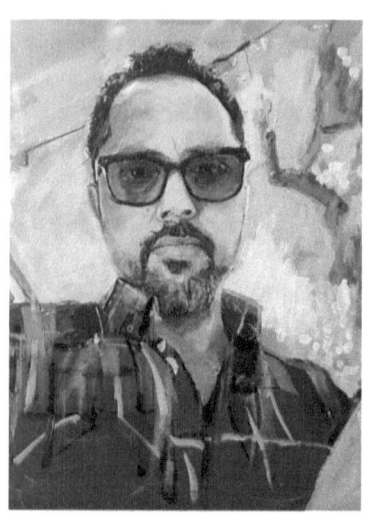

CHAPTER 15 - BRADFORD J. SALAMON

~

ARCADIA, DENNY'S RESTAURANT, 2016

At first, Bradford J. Salamon did not want to meet with me. I wrote him, suggesting a studio visit, and he replied, saying that he is very busy, and that if I wanted to visit with him, I could enroll in his group painting class, which costs hundreds of dollars. Also, the class would entail additional costs because of my out-of-state travel expenses. Many months later, I happen to have an in-depth phone conversation with one of his former pupils, the artist Brian Kern, who resides near Seattle. Brian and I hit it off, and he shares some helpful painting techniques which he learned from Bradford (like how to paint with the destructive/reconstructive method, and how to paint around the edge).

Without my knowledge, Brian later vouches on my behalf to Bradford. Soon afterwards, Bradford contacts me and says that, based upon Brian's positive recommendation, he is willing to meet with me if I am interested. That summer, Bradford and I connect over lunch at the Denny's restaurant in Arcadia. This particular Denny's is iconic because of the gigantic windmill on its roof. We have never met, and my impression of Bradford that day is that he is confident and fired-up about his art, but relaxed at the same time. I order breakfast for our 2:00 lunch. He orders no food and sips his coffee while we chat.

Bradford dives head-first into his backstory: "John, you have to be committed to your art. No matter what happens in your life, you have to be committed. This is how it has been for me. When I was doing work for the Grammy's and my art was selling in my dad's gallery and elsewhere, I had it going on! I had the whole thing — wife, kids, several cars, a big house, and even a few horses. But then I lost it all. I ended up crashing in a storage unit illegally for a good while."

"Then, gradually over the years, I started putting the pieces of the puzzle back together. I got married again, we had our daughters, and we purchased a new house and this studio. And now things are going great, really great! But through it all, I've remained focused on my art. It has seen me through some hard times."

While I eat my eggs, I am struck by the differences between Edgar Arceneaux, who I saw yesterday, and Bradford. Bradford embodies the laid-back, casual Huntington Beach/Orange County vibe. Edgar, on the other hand, manifests the L.A. vibe, which is more assertive, intense, and direct.

A SUBURB, TWENTY MINUTES EAST OF LOS ANGELES, 2017

One year after our lunch at Denny's, I pull up alone to Salamon's studio, which is situated in a guest house behind his main residence. I had some trouble finding it because Google Maps sent me to an incorrect address nearby. I see Bradford watering his lawn by hand outside of his studio. He nods at me as I walk up.

"Hi Bradford. How's it going?" I ask. We shake hands.

"Yeah, dude. Good to see you again. Welcome," he says quietly. His eyes avoid mine. Does he mean to be so distant? Just like I did with Edgar Arceneaux, I offer Bradford a $40 bottle of red wine which I purchased at Ralph's. "A gift," I say.

"I appreciate it man, but you can give it to someone else. I wouldn't drink it." (I later give it to my brother-in-law, Scott.) Bradford and I step inside, and I am immediately startled by a wonderland of creativity before my eyes. I am blown away by his output, and I know that I am only seeing his remaining unsold pieces. As we go in, I see dozens of medium and large-sized paintings hanging on the walls in room after room. Right away, I pick up on a definite chronology in his evolution as a painter -- many of his paintings are significantly better than others. Several are quite great, in fact. A few early ones are overly-literal and too realistic, and I can see experimentation in others. Also, many pencil drawings are tacked up on the walls. On several shelves I see a multitude of valuable brickerbrack, bottles of poison, bottles of nothing, and old metal toys. There is a lone surfboard hanging from the rafters. I also see art books as well, hundreds of them. We continue making our way to the rear of his studio through two more rooms, and then I see it -- *the orange chair*. I recognize it from many photos on Facebook. I know this to be a major node in the L.A. art world, just like Phyllis Lutjean's sofa. As we settle down to chat, I sit in it, but I don't feel a thing.

Bradford lets down his guard, starts smiling, and becomes engaged in conversation. I wonder if he was vetting me again during our first several minutes outside. I know that I am still a stranger to him, but now I think that we may be settling down for some serious art dialogue. Bradford is tall and solidly built. He looks like a middle-aged former surfer/rocker, which he is. His skin is pale, and I presume he keeps out of the sun to avoid any further skin cancer after many years surfing back in the day. He wears dark-framed Ray-Ban glasses (similar to Brett Rubicco and Laddie John Dill). As we talk, he wavers between two polar-opposite modes of engagement: (1) intensely-concentrated listening, and (2) far-off thought, as if he is on Mars, or maybe just super-tired. We scan through some of my artwork from my website on his computer. He comments about a few paintings of celebrities. "Hey John, no more paintings of celebrities. Man, only paint people who you know." I nod.

"Are you aware of Don Bachardy's work?" he asks. "He's great."

"No, not yet," I answer.

"Do you know 'turning the form'? It's like fooling the viewer to see 3D in 2D. David A. Leffel [1931-] did this." Bradford suggests that I become more active on Instagram. He also encourages me to show *process* in my work that I share online. He pauses. "John, how can we work it so that you won't have to continue doing your day job? Perhaps you could paint a bunch of large landscapes. That's what I did years ago. If I had to work a job each day, you know, and punch a clock, I think that I would freakin' kill myself. I have to paint! It's what I'm made to do. I can't do anything else. You have done a ton of paintings recently. I mean, you still have your job, right?" I nod affirmatively. "Well, dammit, John. We need to get you cranking as a full-time artist."

Now he really gets going, brain-storming aloud. "Your next step John, is to start showing your work. You need to decide what you want to be known for. Show everywhere! Show in restaurants where you live. Get work together for an L.A. show, I mean a really solid body of work, like twenty pieces. Make work which doesn't take so long to create, but that is still strong. Do a ton of abstracts in Texas. Maybe do one-hour ones on canvases over and over again on the same topic. Oh - and take a look at Bill Wray's work. Try to get a sense of what he's doing. Man, all I can say is that it is all about *truth*. The biggest thing is to be *sincere*. And from now on, just do paintings; don't make any more sculptures. Give careful consideration to your audience and what you want them to feel. Relate your own uniqueness to your art, and be vulnerable. Do work dealing with what you are currently going through."

I happen to mention that I recently attended his twenty-year survey at The California Heritage Museum in Santa Monica. It was impressive, and it showcased the trajectory and improvement in his work over recent years. I also list the few paintings in his survey which I did not care for. Immediately, his ears prick up, and he becomes keenly interested to learn which ones they were, and my rationale for each of my negative reactions.

Bradford asks me to sit on a bar stool and he begins sketching my portrait. His paper is taped to a board on his easel. He is close to my face, and I feel like I am at the eye doctor. I am uneasy because I am not ever this close to anyone in my personal space, except for my wife. I can feel his warm breath on my face from three feet away. He looks intently into my eyes, but not *at* me.

Bradford makes some small talk while he draws, but he's not really saying much. Only four minutes have passed, and I am bored. Years ago, I underwent many psychological tests because of my memory and listening comprehension problems at work. The psychologists found that I have moderate ADD, and I totally feel it now. So I begin scanning Bradford's studio. It's dark; is it my imagination, or am I perceiving different planes of light? I see thousands of dust particles floating in slender diagonal streams of sunlight which bifurcate the space. I picture the many dozens of artists who have sat here before me. Surely, they must have felt comfortable as I do now, because Bradford is hospitable. His focus is devoted to encouraging others. Where does his benevolent outward orientation come from? He completes his drawing of me (below). He has drawn me with enhanced ruggedness. The image looks like a spawn between Charles Bronson and myself. I like it.

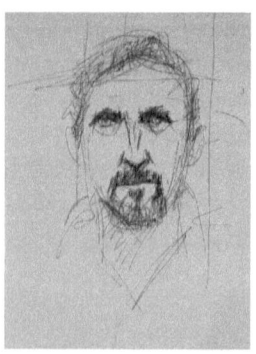

I mention that I have an appointment later that afternoon to meet with the artist Kent Twitchell in Long Beach. "Really?" Bradford intones, somewhat surprised; his eyes squint at me like he's trying to administer a visual lie-detector test with a laser in his retina. "He's a big deal, John. Listen carefully to everything that he says." Julie and I say farewell, and we make our exit. Though we are new acquaintances, in the following seasons Bradford treats me like his apprentice. When I post new works on Facebook, he writes encouraging comments.

A few more years pass, and Bradford has been teaching me to loosen up in my painting. He does this more by his personal example than by his pedagogy. In the past, with my drawings especially, I felt like I had achieved a decent competence in my draftsmanship. However, I was merely drawing like an HP printer; I reproduced what I saw without any soul. Bradford's work, on the other hand, has a lot of soul; consequently, I am learning soulishness in my paintings simply by watching him paint many steps ahead of me.

The following may be an unusual comparison, but Bradford's paintings remind me of the street scenes in Francis Ford Coppola's *The Godfather II*. In this cinematic masterpiece, the camera follows the twenty-something Vito Corleone as he walks through a crowded Little Italy street. Coppola supercedes reality by varying depths of field, and by blurring out large portions of the screen in charcoal obstructions. He mutes colors by adding browns, greys, muddy-oranges, greens, and slushy blacks. He eliminates hard edges with flowers in flowers-stands, fruit in fruit-stands, and hanging laundry on clotheslines which criss-cross back and forth over the street.

Similarly, Salamon's paintings are multi-layered. His edges are nuanced by feathering and by painting around the edge. Salamon does not add nuance merely as a parlor trick, like a monkey playing his street organ. Rather, he creates a series of vertical planes of smoky and sooty atmosphere between the viewer's eyes and the principal objects in the painting. Other more naive artists might simply apply one or two layers of abstraction on top of their realistically painted object.

Bradford, on the other hand, inserts his abstract brush strokes directly inside of his objects, actually stabbing or slicing them into three dimensions. For example, if I were the main figure, he might paint what looks like a layer of nearly transparent sleet bisecting my head. He invites his viewers to forensically peer deep inside of his paintings so that they might understand his process.

THE SAME SUBURB, TWENTY MINUTES EAST OF LOS ANGELES, 2018

Another year has passed and Bradford is reclining in his studio with his feet up on his over-sized desk. This time around, my wife Julie is with me. She and I sit on the other side of his desk. He starts praising my work over and over again, describing it from different perspectives. Much of what he says has to do with my work's future promise, of where my art practice *could* go if I keep at it. I sit there nodding, silently taking it all in because I'm trying not to break his train of thought. He glances over at Julie, and sighs. "Are you friggin' kidding me? Is he hearing anything that I'm saying right now? He looks like he is about to f___-ing kill me right now." Julie looks at me and starts giggling when she notices my rigid stone-face.

She replies to Bradford, laughing, "No, That's just how John is. His face doesn't show it, but what he's thinking right now is, 'This is really cool! I am very excited!'"

I add, "Yeah! What she said!" I repeat her words, "This is really cool! I am very excited!" But when I speak, my words come out flat like Jack Webb in the 1950s *Dragnet* television series. As Julie and I walk out, Bradford makes one last parting comment, "Sh_t, we gotta get you guys back out here to California. John, if

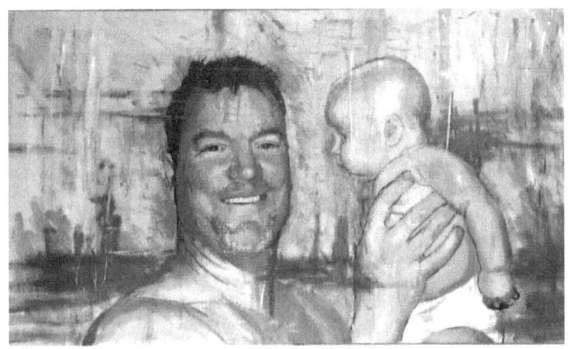

you were here these past few years, you might've already had a solo show by now." We say goodbye; soon after, we fly back to Texas.

———

After this meeting, I send Bradford a few prints of my drawings plus an original self-portrait drawing. He writes me: "I received your drawing and the two prints in the mail; and I really appreciate that nice self portrait! I also got the note that you wrote. That was nice of you to send it. It's nice to know that my ramblings didn't fall on deaf ears. Keep up the great work." A few weeks later, Julie and I purchase a small original oil painting by Bradford of a floor fan. He ships it out to us, and it currently rests on our living room mantle.

NEWPORT BEACH, COASTLINE COMMUNITY COLLEGE, 2019

Tonight is the night of my first group art show in SoCal, curated by Bradford J. Salamon; it has been about five months since I last saw him. Truth be told, months earlier I did have a piece in a group show put on by the

L.A. curator Dulce Stein at Avenue 50 Studio in Los Angeles. But I was unable to fly out to attend that one. See my painting in Dulce's show (see p. 68), which shows Bradford holding his baby daughter.

Bradford invited me to take part in his show, "Kitsch-In-Sync," many months ago, and Julie and I are among the first to arrive. The venue looks fantastic. The architecture of this facility feels like it could have been designed by the famous deceased architect Zaha Hadid.

For the past several weeks, I have been sending out notices via email and Facebook, inviting family and friends from all over L.A. and O.C. This night ends up being a reunion of sorts, and I am humbled. My piece called "Testify," which I entered into the show, is mandated to deal with the theme, *kitsch*, which basically means 'decorative objects in poor taste with a dose of irony.'

At the show, I meet the ubiquitous L.A. art photographer, Eric Minh Swenson, who formerly lived

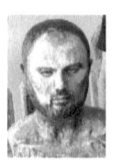

in San Antonio. We shake hands, and he immediately darts away (*my sculpture of him, left*). Next to my painting hangs Leigh Salgado's elegant piece. I do not have an opportunity to meet her. She is married to the writer Mat Gleason, who I write about later in this book. Across the room, I admire the paintings of Regina Jacobsen, Bradford Salamon, and Serena Potter. In my opinion, Ms. Jacobsen's epic painting of a beautiful semi-nude woman steals the show.

I am enjoying myself tonight, but I am embarrassed because of my painting, which is not my best work. It is a still life painting with three figures. It shows a singing

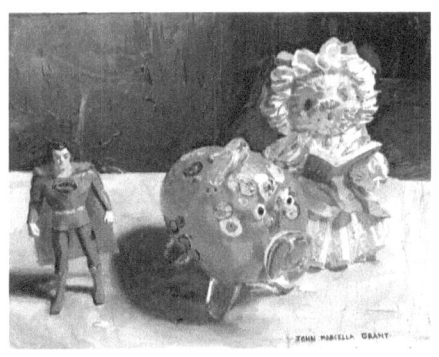

mouse, a red glass pig, and a plastic Superman figure. The work is called "Testify." Here it is (above).

While chitchatting with many family members and friends, a woman approaches and asks me to explain the meaning of my painting. I tell her my thoughts, but my answer seems to displease her, and she quickly walks away.

A while later, I meet Brent Higginson, who sells Bradford J. Salamon's prints near the Huntington Beach Pier. He is encouraging to me and praises my work. Higginson introduces me to the artist and author Gordon T. McClelland, who writes extensively about California orange box labels, among other topics. When I return to Texas, I call McCelland and interview him about his career for about half an hour over the phone. Next, I meet Michael Sewell, an Orange County-based actor and Facebook friend whose work I have long admired. Before the exhibition, I invited him to attend my show on a whim. Other L.A. artists who I invited via email declined to attend, saying the hour-long drive from L.A. to Newport Beach was too long.

My childhood best friend, Joel Berryhill, is here. He plays in the surfer band, the Surfaris. (His dad, Bob Berryhill, was one of their original members.) My college best friend, Victor Kreider, and his wife Tamira show up as well. Many years ago, he was known as "Elliot

Wild" when he played in his rock band in many venues on Sunset Boulevard. Weeks later on the phone, Victor exhorts me to dress better and to style my hair more modishly for my next show. I guess friends are allowed to say stuff like that.

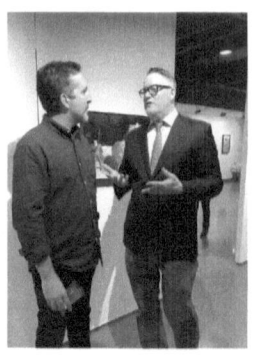

I am grateful to Bradford J. Salamon (right) for including me in this show; he is a magnanimous host. I am forty-six-years-old, but still one of the youngest artists to participate. I join in to pose for a group photo with about twenty of the other artists (see below). It is a noisy group, and many of them have their arms around each other. As we smile together, I am set off a bit at the lower-right-hand corner.

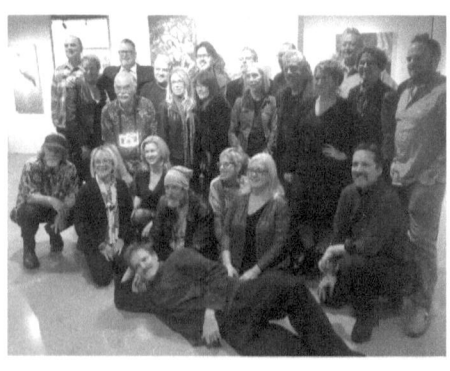

The night is over so quickly, and I wonder if it was just another baby-step forward. Am I any farther along in my art path? Is this all just an expensive exercise in futility? Am I really an artist at all? Later on that evening, as I lie in bed in the guest room at my parents' house, I wonder about the overall content of my work. What am I really trying to say? The singer/

songwriter Bob Dylan once said that, "An artist has got to be constantly in a state of becoming." I know where I want my painting to get to, but it may take me thirty years to do it. With each passing year, I can see my technique and content steadily improving. I wonder if I will live long enough for my art to get to where I want it to be. I don't have time to ruminate over this for too long, because Bradford continues to push me forward.

About four months go by, and Bradford visits the SFMOFA with his buddy, the well-known painter Bill Wray. Bradford shares photos of their trek on Facebook; I see that they view many Diebenkorn paintings. Recently, I have been reading about Diebenkorn (1922-1993) in John Seed's new book, *My Art World.* According to Seed, Diebenkorn was a pretty straight-forward, squarish guy. Seed writes, "Diebenkorn isn't a good candidate for a full biography as his bourgeois and stable personal life leaves little to gossip about."

Subsequently, just two weeks ago, Bradford suggested that I purchase a book by Fairfield Porter called *Art In Its Own Terms.* Porter (1907-1975), according to the introduction in his book "was known as one of the best painters in America. His own opinion was that he was a stronger critic." It seems that he viewed his writing to be just as important as his painting.

An artist who is squarish?

Another artist who writes?

I think Bradford, whether he knows it or not, may be introducing me to a few more artists in my tribe. The only problem is that my tribe seems to be made up predominantly of dead artists. That's a depressing thought. But I am very much alive. In addition to being a square writer, I am also *sincere* and *earnest*, qualities looked down upon by many in today's art world. In fact, Bradford Salamon describes me with these two terms in his blurb on the back cover of this book, *Discovering the L.A. Art World*. I ask the writer and gallerist Mat Gleason about these two qualities. He writes, "These two traits leave one vulnerable to mockery. The whole of the creative arts has a soft spot and it is these. The hacks aim straight for this target. That is where they come for you."

This makes me want to rebel against the hacks, whomever they may be.

CHAPTER 16 - KENT TWITCHELL

~

LONG BEACH, ABOUT TWO MILES FROM THE
QUEEN MARY, 2017

After spending part of this afternoon with Bradford Salamon in his studio in the Inland Empire, I arrive alone in Long Beach, the city of my birth. The setting yellow sun blasts through huge ficuses and stubby palm trees across the street from Twitchell's four story apartment building. I am surprised to see that he lives here. I half-expected him to live in a luxurious pad somewhere else. I buzz him on my wife's cell phone (which we share). A moment later, Twitchell emerges from his building's main lobby to the sidewalk out front where we hold our first meeting. He may be L.A.'s most eminent muralist. We meet and shake hands.

Mr. Twitchell was born in 1942 in Lansing, Michigan. In 1966, he moved to Los Angeles. He earned his BA at Cal State L.A. Subsequently, he earned his MFA at Otis College of Art and Design, in Los Angeles. Since 1971, he has painted nearly thirty murals in the greater

L.A. area. Some writers even describe him as "The Godfather of Street Art."

One of Twitchell's large murals depicts the famous SoCal artist Ed Ruscha. Twitchell has long admired Ruscha because he sees him as an artist who really *got* *L.A.* Twitchell is also famous for his painting adjacent to the Hollywood Freeway entitled *The Freeway Lady.* (It was illegally destroyed in 1986.) As Twitchell painted, he would work on multiple projects simultaneously. He reiterates this in a note to me, when he writes, "I work best when I can do two major projects at the same time."

In 1983, his friend, the artist Alonzo Davis (1942-) came up with the idea for painting murals for the 1984 Olympics. For this occasion, Twitchell painted his friend, the artist Lita Albuquerque (1946-) as Mary from the Bible, and his other friend, the artist Jim Morphesis (1948-) as Jesus. Later on, after these two murals were vandalized, the State of California commissioned a professional art conservator to transfer them to a new location. This was done using the Strappo technique developed in Italy to remove ancient frescoes. This allowed both murals to be virtually vibrated off the walls and moved to a new location where they remain to the present day.

According to the conceptual artist Gary Lloyd (1943-), who Twitchell also admires, Twitchell is meticulous. In fact, it takes him a year or more to complete a single piece. Jim Morphesis (in Eric Minh Swenson's YouTube video, *Kent Twitchell: Guardians, Part 1 of 4*), says of Twitchell that he "does work of a spiritual nature, and doesn't try to hide it. Yeah. In this town that is very subversive."

While standing with me on his front sidewalk, Kent dives into a technical explanation of his process. His technique, in which he paints with various shades or values on Polytab, is complex. Next, Kent recommends art supplies to me. For most of his early drawings he used Ticonderoga pencils, 1, 2, 2 1/2, 3 and 4's. Lately he has added Tombow Mono pencils from Japan (sometimes Tombow Mono 100) and Palomino Blackwing in their three grades. He also likes Tombow and Blackwing erasers. As we converse, he seems guarded and distant, just like Bradford Salamon was during our first meeting together.

Like Luis Serrano, Kent studied under Charles White. Kent explains why we cannot go upstairs to his studio, but I now forget his reasoning. Later on, I would understand that he was only being careful.

After I email him an amazing pencil drawing by another artist, Kent writes back, "I MUCH prefer your work. This is just the armed-over photo-realism of the early 1970s. It shows commitment and patience. But you have soul." His comment here refers to my figurative-realist pencil drawings and paintings, and I feel encouraged.

LONG BEACH, 2018

For my next visit with Kent a year later at "The Library, A Coffee House" on East Broadway in Long Beach, I bring my secret weapon — my wife Julie. Artists really seem to like her (as did Mark Bradford, Bradford Salmon, Laddie John Dill, and today, hopefully Kent Twitchell). I tend to be a stick-in-the-mud artist who makes some decent work. But, fortunately for me, Julie is great at translating the essence of what I am trying to say during our conversations with other artists. (She'll remark, "What he's trying to say is _____." And the artist will reply, "Well, why didn't he just say that?")

It is interesting to me that Julie is adept at something for which she has little fondness. By this I mean that she would rather *not* go on many of my wild-goose-chase art adventures. I think that from her perspective, this may be because of four reasons: First, in her mind, each visit seems like a sales-pitch. Second, my studio visits feel somewhat futile to her. In fact, she has wondered aloud to me before, "What have these meetings accomplished?" This is because she is a realist and I am a dreamer. Third, she does not particularly enjoy meeting with strangers. She is outgoing with people whom she already knows, but not so much with complete unknowns. And fourth, Julie is not an artist; and artists are not those to whom she would naturally gravitate. But ironically, she did choose to marry me; but when we got together twenty-five years ago, I was not yet making much art.

During this visit with Kent, the vibe between us seems different. I don't know if this is because I brought Julie along, but Kent appears more comfortable this time around. We steer clear of scientific art talk, and he and Julie hit it off. As the two of them converse, I study Kent's features. I think to myself, "The lighting in here is perfect for a portrait." So I take some photos of him for a future painting which I will complete when we return to Texas (below).

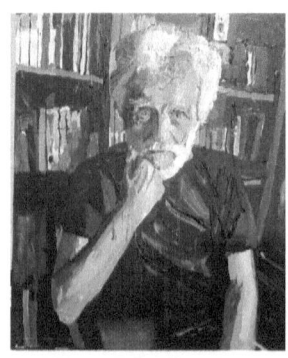

As I snap photos, I notice that Kent is powerfully built and short in stature. He has an impressive mane of white hair, a wild beard, piercing eyes (like an Old Testament prophet), and a strong brow ridge. After recounting his days in the Air Force in London, and his exceptional level of physical fitness back in the day, he punches his gut, grins, and mutters, "Boy, I still got it!" He reminisces about his friendship with Clayton Moore, the actor who played the Lone Ranger on television. Kent was in awe of him, and then they actually became good friends. In the late '60s, Kent began making street art. He quickly demonstrates to us how he draws with pencils sometimes with swirls (below) rather than with diagonal hatches:

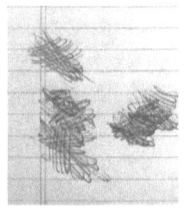

After our stimulating conversation with Kent, Julie and I walk back to our car, and we discover a parking ticket on our windshield. Several days later, we receive a nice email from Kent which reads, "I really enjoyed meeting both of you… You are a source of inspiration to me seeing you do such powerful work… Julie, you are a treasure. I'm thinking that John fell into the gravy boat when he found you."

Later, after I mail him an original self-portrait drawing, he writes a postcard which says, "John, Thanks for the self-portrait. I will treasure it. - God bless you both!"

I am curious about Kent's process. I write him, "When you do art, are your thought-processes tangential? Or do you come up with a theme and work around it?"

He replies, "Since 1971, I have been interested in drawing and painting American cultural heroes. I have no interest in 99% of famous Hollywood people. I suppose that my techniques have been more tangential, but not the content of my efforts."

I realize I did not express my question clearly, so I clarify: "How about in the midst of when you are painting -- are you following a preset theme which you have chosen (like when one writes an essay), and then you build up around the theme . . . or do you follow whims sometimes?"

Kent answers: "Painting my murals is more pre-organized than doing art therapy or pretending [that] I'm an expressionist. But [while] painting in the studio, I do explore surprises that come up." Just like in medicine, there is both an art and science to Kent's work. He really is a genius. *(My recent painting of another L.A. muralist, Jaase Jay, below.)*

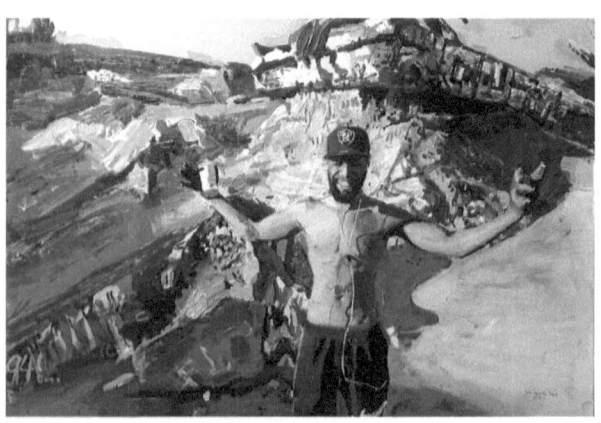

CHAPTER 17 - HUNG VIET NGUYEN

~

TORRANCE, 2018

I arrive early at Hung Viet Nguyen's house. We are Facebook art friends, and via Facebook, I have set up today's studio visit. I arrive about twenty minutes early, so I wait in my car listening to the radio. I notice his wife get into her car and drive away. After a while, I get out of my car and knock on his front door. Hung looks just like he does in his Facebook photos. He has a warm smile, long grey hair, and a round face. He stretches out his hand and welcomes me. His hospitality is palpable. We go inside, and I see that the walls of his living room are overflowing with art from many L.A. art friends. The far wall contains an impressive collection of marathon running medals bound together, and some vintage photos of Hung running in races.

"Hello, John! How are you? So good to to see you! Come in! Are you hungry? I made some steak, and I have some red wine ready." It is early, about eleven AM. "Do you drink?" I nod affirmatively. "Here, have some. How was your trip? You came all the way from Texas?"

"Yes, we live there now. But I am originally from Seal Beach, and we are here visiting family. Thank you so much for having me."

"Hey, John, I love your work. Wow, you have a way with the brush, and with your pencil drawings too."

"Thank you, Hung. I am learning."

"No, man! You got it now! You are so good! Here! Eat more. Are you hungry?" We eat some thin lightly-seasoned slices of steak, and drink a little red wine. I take a few snapshots of Hung which I will later use as source images for his portrait (below).

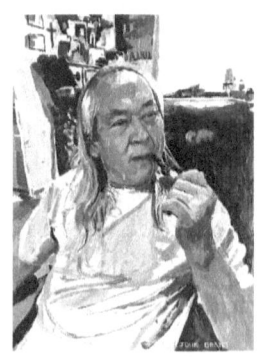

Hung leads me out on his side driveway, which connects to his garage studio behind his house. This is the exact same setup which I saw at Edgar Arceneaux's place. Hung calmly explains, "Yeah, man. This is where I do my work." He begins pulling down canvases one by one from a five-foot-deep wooden rack suspended in his garage. The steady improvement in his paintings through the years is unmistakable. His is a very similar evolution to what I saw in Bradford Salamon's studio. I am amazed at how much Hung's paintings have improved, even within the past year or two. As he starts speaking, he begins teaching me from his bag of tricks. Class is in session, and I have *so* much to learn.

"John, see these colors?" He holds one of his early works, a painting from many years ago. "See how I painted with paint straight out of the tube? Too many primary colors! This is not good, John. I notice that you still do that. You need more greys, browns, muddy-yellows and oranges. Also, do you spend enough time on your work? I don't think so. I work on these new ones for months. I think that you need to take your time, John. Spend more time on each individual work."

I am transfixed by his current in-process painting on his easel. It reminds me of Shangri-La because it depicts a collection of waterfalls, cliffs, and gardens. The composition is perfect and his color choices are more than perfect - brown-greens... grey-blues. His brush-strokes resemble plowed lines in a field, deeply textured, so deep, in fact, that many of the ridges cast their own small shadows. On his canvas, I detect a tiny swimming figure painted in one of the pools. There are some small words scrawled in the water, and they are difficult to make out. Do they say "Romeo and Juliet"? I think that they do.

L.A. CONVENTION CENTER, DOWNTOWN LOS ANGELES, 2019

A long while later, at the L.A. Art Show, Hung and I cross paths again. I can tell he is preoccupied with filming an art video, so we take a quick snapshot together (see p. 83) and go our own separate ways.

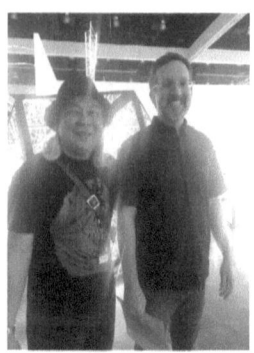

As Julie, our older son Nathan (age nineteen), and I are exiting the L.A. Convention Center, we meet the well-known artist Chaz Guest (1961-). I introduce myself, and he listens attentively as Nathan describes his diverse interests in rock climbing, entrepreneurship, and coffee. Mr. Guest is impeccably dressed in a fancy sports coat and a scarf. He carries himself with a strong presence, and he most definitely looks like a professional artist. (*my acrylic paintings of Nathan, below left, and Tish and Greg Laemmle, Hung's supporters, below right*)

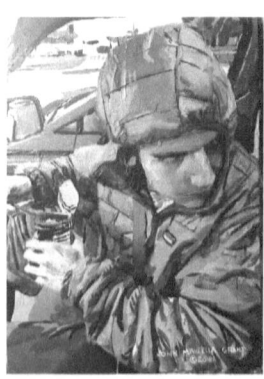
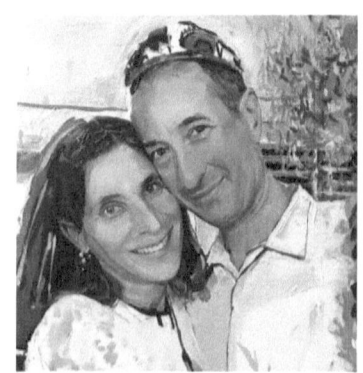

CHAPTER 18 - LUIS AND ANA
SERRANO

~

LOS ANGELES, 2018

Julie and I visited the LACMA (L.A. County Museum of Art) this afternoon. Now we are driving a few miles south to meet with Luis and Ana Serrano for dinner, and we pull up to their quaint house. I think that they are the only two art figures who I will meet during my studio tours whose hospitality equals Hung's. Luis opens the door with a big smile. "Welcome, John and Julie! How are you guys? We are so glad that you could make it!" Julie and I walk in and sit down in their living room under an unpainted, shallow, barrel-vaulted ceiling, and one by one, Luis describes many of the original artworks which hang on his walls.

Ana steps out from the kitchen. "Hello! So nice to meet you both!" Savory aromas waft out of their kitchen. We enjoy an amazing home-cooked meal and good wine with Luis, Ana, and their son on a long picnic table in their backyard. The abundant variety of flora and fauna in the space is so impressive that it almost feels Edenic.

Luis begins sharing stories about his path as an artist. Their son departs, and we transfer our art discussion back into the living room. I share an idea that I view the various art media of drawing, painting, and sculpture to be hierarchical, from least to greatest. Ana disagrees, suggesting that my hypothesis denigrates the medium of drawing. I begin to re-evaluate my supposition.

Luis mentions his friend, the well-known artist Kerry James Marshall, who grew up in South-Central Los Angeles and now lives in Chicago, Illinois. He graduated from Otis College of Art and Design in 1978. Luis and Marshall studied together under Charles White (whose work, as I write this, is being featured at LACMA). Like Mark Bradford, Marshall was a recipient of the MacArthur Foundation "genius grant" in 1997. Marshall's work set a sales record in 2018 when a single piece sold for $21 million.

Luis informs me about many other great artists such as Yasuo Kuniyoshi (1889-1953), Dan McCleary (1952-) (his friend), Chaim Soutine (1893-1943), Scott Hess (1955-), Georgio de Chirico (1888-1978), Emil Kosa Jr. (1903-1968), and R.B. Kitaj (1932-2007). He also refers to the writer Joseph Campbell (1904-1987), and his significant impact on artists. As Luis describes these luminaries, he is effusive. He suggests that I check out *Claude Glass*, which is a sort of black stone mirror which many landscape artists use in their work.

Luis' principal studio space these days is simply the outdoors in nature. In his current works, he depicts landscapes with gouache, ocher and charcoal, or pencil over and over again. Many of his landscape paintings are executed with exquisite detail and realism. Luis places equal importance on both pencil marks *and* erasures, and this is very curious to me. In a fashion not unlike J. Michael Walker's, Luis seems to enjoy a harmonious balance in life between family, work, nature, food, friends, teaching, travel, and making art (not necessarily in that order). Luis received both his BFA and MFA from the Otis Art Institute in L.A. Similar to Kent Twitchell, he is a mentor at the Laguna College of Art + Design (LCAD).

I mail Luis an original pencil portrait which I drew of him (below).

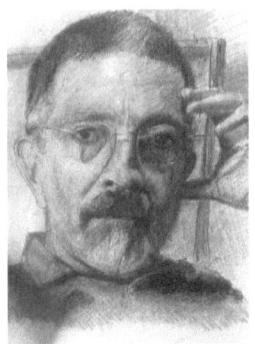

Below are a few of my newest acrylic paintings of two artists who I hope to meet in L.A. in the summer of 2020 (Narsiso Martinez and Karrie Ross).

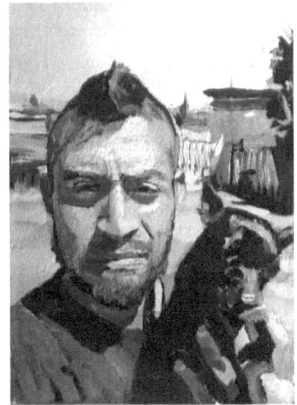
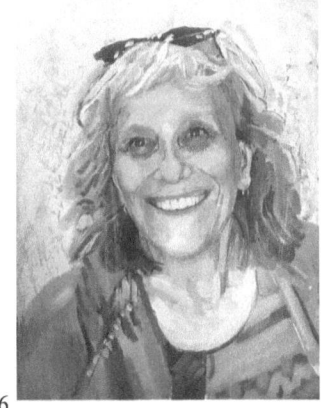

CHAPTER 19 - JOSE LOZANO

~

COLLEGE STATION, 2019

About six months after visiting with Luis and Ana Serrano in California, I remove a lid off of a recently delivered cardboard shipping tube in our College Station, Texas home, and out tumbles an original drawing by the SoCal artist Jose Lozano, in addition to four color laminated prints of his hand-drawn color greeting cards (below). This feels like Christmas morning — for an artist.

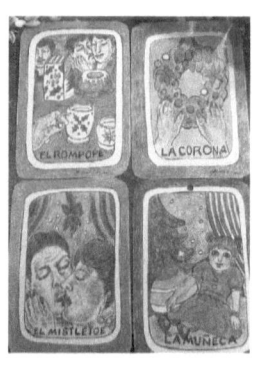

One card depicts a couple kissing. Previously, I had mailed Jose an original pencil drawing which I drew of him. In the sketch, I modified his face to look like Dick Tracy. I accentuated his cheek bones and made him look more rugged. We have never met in person, but we have become art friends on Facebook. Just this past week on Facebook, Jose posted photos of his artwork being applied to the sides of a multistory building in L.A. (at La Plaza de Cultura y Artes). It looks impressive in its magnified scale, content, and execution. (*My acrylic painting of Jose, below*)

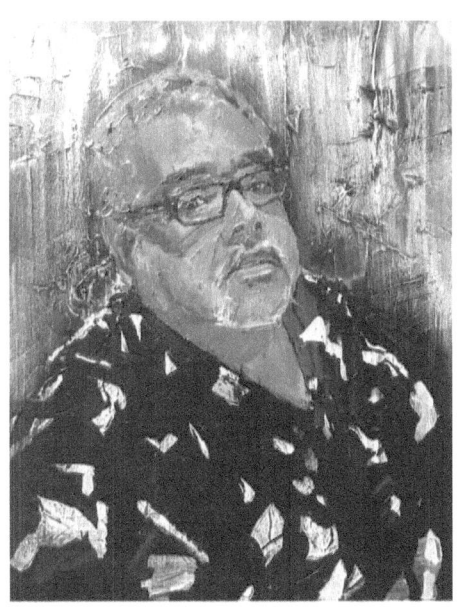

CHAPTER 20 - STEFAN SIMCHOWITZ,
MICHAEL LORENZO PORTER, AND
MAT GLEASON

~

In my opinion, the two greatest non-artist minds in the L.A. art world are Stefan Simchowitz and Mat Gleason. Stefan Simchowitz (A.K.A. Simco) is a dynamic Stanford-educated art collector and writer based in Beverly Hills. Mat Gleason is a tenacious L.A. City College-educated gallerist, curator, and writer based in L.A's Chinatown. I have approached Simco multiple times with samples of my work on Facebook. If anything, Simco is accessible online, but we have not yet met in person. The two biggest influencers in the SoCal region art scene on Facebook, in my opinion, also happen to be Simco and Mat Gleason. The biggest influencer in the national art world in my view is the writer Jerry Saltz.

In my efforts to connect with prominent art figures online, I begin to view Facebook as a *complex puzzle*, rather than a social media platform. I try to identify the most important element in all of Facebook. I believe it to be *the influencer,* and I am definitely *not* an influencer. An influencer is basically the most popular person in a group, just like in high school. For years, I used the *People You May Know* feature on Facebook. (It no longer exists.) It was a subset of the "friends" window. I begin adding friends who were friends of art world influencers. At one point, I send Simco a black-and-white image of a pencil drawing which I drew of seven women from days of old. Simco responds, "I like. Email me high-res image please." I send the image to him (below). Then I wait…no response.

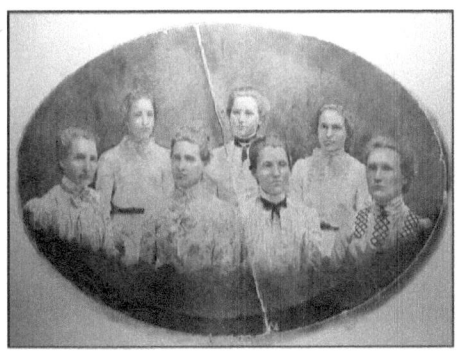

Later on, I send Simco more images of my work. A high school acquaintance of mine, Hartwell Brown (who, like Simco, is a Stanford alum), writes a glowing letter to him on my behalf. Simco writes me back, "I am also not interested in the work." The door is closed, at least for the time being.

Since I'm not having any luck with Simco "running up the middle," I decide to call an audible and run a "Bang 8 Post." The "Bang 8 Post" calls for the receiver to run seven steps straight downfield before breaking inside at an angle. If I cannot bond with Simco, then I will interact with those around him, and perhaps engage with him directly at a later date. Around the end of July, 2018, I read an insightful article about Simco by the writer Michael Lorenzo Porter in the online *HyperAllergic* newsletter entitled "The Notorious Stefan Simco on Art Dealing, Social Media, and Faith in Art." Porter's writing style is captivating and accessible. He and I connect on Facebook Messenger, and after some time, he interviews me over the phone for an upcoming article. With his breezy confidence, he reminds me of Lando Calrissian from *The Empire Strikes Back*. In fact, he's a great foil for my uptight self. I can imagine Porter delivering Lando's classic line to Leia, "Hello — what have we here?" Interestingly, as we interact, I end up receiving some off-the-cuff advice from Porter about how to relax and be in the moment during an interview. I enjoy continuing to learn tidbits like this, unrelated to art, but still along my art pilgrimage. In the past year or so, life has intervened, and Porter has had to take care of personal business, postponing his article about me.

Out of Simco's full stable of creatives, the artist Marc Horowitz is my favorite. He seems to have fully transitioned from his humorous and ironic work early on to more serious and grounded work today (similar to the career arc of the seasoned actor Tom Hanks). He also happens to be my lone doppelgänger in the L.A. art world; he looks like a taller version of me. As it turns out, I met Marc last week at his solo show in Houston at the Jonathan Hopson Gallery (September, 2019).

In March of 2019, I write Simco again: "I would enjoy seeing you do an art talk/debate with Mat Gleason (perhaps with the writer Carolina A. Miranda moderating)." No response. I know when it is time for me to move on, and the time is now. Subsequently, I write Gleason suggesting a debate between him and Simco: "You should challenge Stefan Simchowitz to an 'art battle' just like Bradford Salamon's and Bill Wray's art battles on YouTube. But instead of painting, you could debate each other about hot current art topics."

Gleason responds: "He's terrified of me, blocked me across social media...He's a rare bird in the art world, not many people [like him] gravitate towards art. So the debate would basically be a study in extremes of personality..."

I write, "He graduated from Stanford."

Gleason responds with a witty, derisive slam against Stanford. If the Simco/Gleason debate were a Rocky movie, Gleason might be victorious because he is the underdog, and underdogs are usually crowd-favorites. As evidenced in our written correspondence (above), the door of communication between Gleason and myself is cracked open ever-so-slightly.

Gleason is currently one of my favorite art writers, along with John Seed. Gleason writes in an accessible style similar to the deceased *L.A. Times* sports writer of the 1980s, who I grew up reading, named Jim Murray (1919-1998). I am curious about Gleason's writing process, so I ask him, "Do you ever work so hard on your art (I mean, your writing), that you get burned out, and run out of juice for a while? If so, what do you do to recharge?"

He replies, "I just watch TV for a year and then the juice is back." Gleason is the publisher and owner of the *Coagula Art Journal* (formerly in print, and now solely available online). He has been writing about art intensely in the *Coagula Art Journal* since 1992. He writes with a punk aesthetic because he comes from that particular music scene. He also runs his own gallery, Coagula Curatorial, with an egalitarian, welcoming, community sensibility. His gallery, for regulars, is a place of inclusion... for outsiders, not so much (*Since the first printing of this book, Gleason has closed his gallery.*).

In the past, Gleason was a transgressor who rebelled against the art world establishment. But recently, as his gallery has thrived, he has become a gatekeeper of sorts for the L.A. art world, at least for the cheap seats. On a personal level, Gleason has been dealing with major health issues for most of his life. He describes them on YouTube by saying, "I have a weird heart condition." Though Gleason used to go out many nights a week to be part of the art scene, and to be *in the know* to be able to write authoritatively about the L.A. art world, he currently concentrates on his gallery. He has to man the store, so he cannot possibly see everything around town.

These days, his favorite museum in SoCal is the Norton Simon Museum in Pasadena. In a YouTube interview, Gleason turned me on to the Frederick R. Weisman Art Foundation, a fantastic collection housed in a mansion in the Holmby Hills District of Los Angeles. Two years ago, Julie and I made an online reservation and took the tour. Their collection is beyond amazing. But sadly, as I write this book, the Weisman Foundation's website has been taken down. I digress. Let's rewind to my first interactions with Gleason.

DALLAS, TEXAS, 2015

Today, I am attending the Dallas Art Fair with one of my College Station, Texas art friends, Renzo Binda. He started out as a photographer; he has since transitioned into painting. We met at the Subway sandwich shop by my house in Texas where he used to work nine to five. On many days, I would go there, order a sandwich, and we would converse about our favorite artists such as Jean Michel Basquiat, Lucian Freud and Alice Neel. These days, Renzo is creating a lexicon of symbols in his paintings, much like a personalized visual alphabet.

At the fair, Renzo notices the actor Tobey Maguire, and chases after him down the crowded convention hallway, yelling, "Tobey, Tobey!" Renzo and I separate, and I make my way alone to the Coagula Curatorial booth, hoping to cross paths with Gleason. As I walk along, I silently rehearse my "elevator speech." Suddenly, Gleason is right there, standing before me. He is of short-to-medium height, average weight, pale, with grey hair. He looks tired, and extremely bored. I introduce myself, "I am John Marcella Grant." Why do I sound out of breath? "I am a big fan of your writing. I am an L.A. artist currently living in Texas." I hand him my handheld portfolio and say, "Here is some of my work." I take a quick breath, lift up my gaze, and notice that he is staring at somebody else over my shoulder.

His body language reads, "Yeah, yeah, you knucklehead. I am trying to sell some art here. Can't you see that?" Later, I would watch many of his YouTube videos online — and in one, he explains that art shows are for dealers and collectors alone, and not for artists. He says that artists should remain in their studios and just make their work. I remember now that Mark Bradford uttered those very same words to Julie. Gleason flips through my book for two seconds and shoves it back into my hands. "Great, thanks," he mumbles. He turns ninety degrees, shuffles away, and he is gone.

"Well that was disappointing," I think to myself. "Six hour round-trip drive all for nothing." Actually, it was not all for nothing. In just four short years, it is

Gleason himself who personally challenges me to write this book, *Discovering the L.A. Art World*.

DOWNTOWN LOS ANGELES, 2017

Generally, when we visit Chinatown, my family and I execute the same drill. We drive from Seal Beach (taking the 405 to the 110) to the Disney Concert Hall in downtown L.A. We go there for the safe and convenient subterranean parking. When you visit, enter the Disney Hall parking garage from the street level on West Second Street, in between the Disney Hall and the Broad. After parking, ride several red escalators back up to the ground level, and cross the street to the fantastic Broad Museum, which resembles an enormous white cheese grater sent back in time from the future. We walk through the entire venue, which has free admission. Be sure to make reservations online ahead of time so that you can wait in the shorter line. The works of Mark Bradford and Jean-Michel Basquiat steal the show. I see some of Koons' work upstairs, and I very much dislike it - not because of its extravagant value, but because it feels sleazy and dated, perfectly symbolizing 80's consumer excess.

Subsequently, we cross the street to the MOCA (Museum of Contemporary Art). It looks like a building from 1986, which it is. I buy a single ticket for myself, to be frugal. I just read online that their price of admission is now free. I do a speedy loop through the MOCA. I like it, I guess. I realize that the MOCA was a very big deal back in the 1980s, but some of their Warhols and Rauschenbergs are yellowing with time. The MOCA is like left-over Domino's pizza — if you're hungry, it will fill you up, but it doesn't taste so good. Many times it feels like the curators are attempting to overly-compensate for their aging collection with R-rated racy or ultra-violent contemporary fare just to add shock value.

Two art figures featured in this book, are currently on the MOCA Board of Directors (Mark Grotjahn and Mark Bradford). Furthermore, the MOCA recently hired a new senior curator, Mia Locks. One secret to invigorate your visit is to track down Basquiat's work *Six Crimee*, if it happens to be on display. It depicts six figures with halos on three panels. I don't fully understand why, but this piece pulses with energy. I have spent a lot of time with this painting, just soaking it in. It has a similar vibe to Van Gogh's small portrait of his mother at the Norton Simon Museum. Both pieces are painted in a Colgate toothpaste green, and when I am in their presence, they both feel electric.

Next, the five of us take a short walk to the Angels Flight funicular railway. It costs one dollar each way per ticket. (Don't scrimp on tickets and take the stairs — They reek of pee.) The train delivers us down Bunker Hill to the Grand Central Market, where we buy tortas (huge sandwiches made with fajitas, avocados, and tomatoes, on freshly-baked buns). After lunch, we take the Angels Flight back up the hill and walk to the bike racks across the street from the MOCA. There, my son Shane and I rent bicycles from an automated kiosk to ride to Chinatown, about half a mile away. As we pedal up and down the steep hills, I struggle, and realize I have been painting too much lately, and I am out of shape. My son cruises along effortlessly. (He is eighteen, and runs cross-country and plays soccer at his school.) In Chinatown, Shane and I weave through teeming throngs of tourists on our way to Mat Gleason's small gallery (see my drawing, next page).

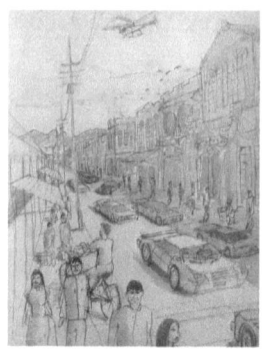

We turn left and take a fortuitous short-cut behind the tourist shops. We zoom by a wide-open entrance of a large temple where we see a crowd of Asian seniors doing Tai-Chi in the courtyard in beautiful and graceful synchronized choreography. As we ride closer to Gleason's gallery, I am amazed by how much Chinatown has remained the same over the recent decades. I am an expert on Chinatown's history because I watched *T.J. Hooker*. In one episode, William Shatner's character tracks down an arms dealer, and the trail leads him straight to Chinatown, where he discovers a network of underground tunnels used for smuggling arms and contraband. Chinatown was also featured in *Lethal Weapon 4* with Mel Gibson.

We continue pedaling, and I cycle past the well-known photographer Osceola Refetoff as he walks from a nearby parking lot. I recognize him from Facebook, but we have never met. Also from social media, I know that he and Mat Gleason are acquaintances. Shane and I finally arrive at Coagula Curatorial, and I lug my rental bike inside because I lack a bike lock. Meanwhile, Shane continues weaving around the nearby galleries and stores outside. Gleason is in his rear office hovel, which resembles a closet. He shuffles out, and his back is stooped. I introduce myself (it has been two years since our brief Dallas interaction), and he says, "Oh yeah, I think I recognize you from Facebook. Good to see you." He does a 180, and ambles back into his den. I realize this "greet-and-walk-away" routine is his modus operandi. I remember back to when one of the other art figures in this book warned me to stay away from Gleason because he would steamroll over my mild, easy-going demeanor. But I don't give up easily. I have friends who are similar to him — opinionated, sharp-tongued, and they act like tough guys.

He has left me standing there all alone, and Coagula Curatorial's interior is telling. It is a single, medium-sized room, with white walls, a small wine cooler (see, Ling's Wine and Beer Market), and a checkerboard floor. It couldn't be any more different from the Gagosian Gallery in Beverly Hills, or from the Blum and Poe Gallery in Culver City (both relatively grand and fancy). I know that crowds do not visit for Gleason's kumbayas. Rather, they flock here for connectivity (for locals who are hard-working artists), for authenticity, and for the celebration of art for art's sake in a bullshit-free zone.

While I stand there, I feel homesick for Southern California. (It was where I spent my first thirty-one years.) I desire to move back to my hometown, Seal Beach, and attend the shindigs at Coagula. But I know I am still an outsider in the L.A. art world. And we are financially strapped. While I day-dream, I try to imagine how we could move back to SoCal. But the math just doesn't add up, especially in terms of rent or mortgage costs.

Later online, I begin a back-and-forth dialogue with Gleason: "How are most blue collar artists you know able to afford the crazy rents/mortgages in L.A. or Orange Counties?"

He replies, "Doesn't exist. Rich parents or GTFO... Or marry well!"

I begin to wonder if there is any "there there" at his gallery? Is there any substance? So, I write Gleason again, "So much of the lower and mid-level art scene in L.A. reminds me of the singing competition 'The Voice' . . . a lot of hubbub, but not many skyrocketing artists."

He answers: "It is like community theater down the street from the Hollywood studios. Only thing [that] I can think of is that these systems all eventually collapse. It is different now from how it was in the recent past - and it will be different in the future; sometimes [this is] the only thing that keeps me going." Even though I currently live half a continent away from Gleason, and we are not friends, he (in his writing and YouTube videos) has unknowingly inspired me to work diligently in my art. I suppose I view him as a player-coach of sorts, because he is definitely in the game. Therefore, I write him a short note of thanks which reads:

"Reading the obit which you posted compelled me to write you a short note of thanks before I forget, and never write at all. I don't know you, but thanks for sharing your fun, dry art wit, thereby encouraging me to press on in my art pilgrimage. Thanks for writing with smarts, and for being an independent thinker... It is fun to observe from afar someone like yourself using his gifts to do exactly what he was made to do. Finally, your love and devotion to your wife, parents, and your friends sheds light into the often dark art world. I can't help but notice how you encourage others through your classes, clinics, shows, museum tours, dinners, etc. Have a great day!"

He responds, "This means a lot! I can have a polarizing effect with what I put out there, and I get shunned for speaking my truth a bit. So, it is nice to read this. Made my week!" In May of 2018, I paint an acrylic portrait of Gleason (below), and send a photo of it to him via Facebook.

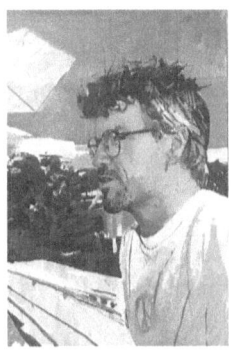

He writes: "I love it. I wish I had worn a different shirt that day 20+ years ago! But, WOW! What an amazing rendering! Can I post this on Facebook (with credit to you of course)?"

Later on, I write a review of Gleason's gallery, Coagula Curatorial, on Facebook: "Gleason is the Aristophanes of L.A.'s blue collar art world. Aristophanes' pen was feared as he ridiculed famous Athenians. Gleason's pen is sharpened by his intimate knowledge of L.A.'s contemporary art scene. Not only does Gleason offer biting critiques of many Southland artists (both low and famous high-brow ones), he breaks bread with them as well. Crowds attend art shows at Coagula. The sparseness and austerity of this tiny gallery contrasts with its host's encouragement and hospitality, which draws artists there in droves."

He responds, "I'm flattered, thanks!"

After consolidating my various interactions with Gleason (above), I see that I have engaged in some fawning obsequiousness in our give-and-takes. Oh well... so be it.

DOWNTOWN LOS ANGELES, LOS ANGELES CONVENTION CENTER, 2019

Julie, Shane (our 18-year-old son), and I visit the L.A. Art Show today. As an aside, Shane is a vlogger (shanesvlogs) on YouTube. One of his latest videos on the app called "Tik-Tok" recently garnered four million views. Sometimes I wonder if, after all of my art adventures, maybe Shane is the one who is actually destined for greatness. This would be similar to the dynamic between Picasso and his father, who was an artist, professor, and a curator. His father made paintings of birds in the marketplace and sold them for a pittance, especially when compared to his son's future astronomical art prices.

Julie and I meander over to Gleason's booth, and I have yet another interaction with Gleason just like I did in Dallas back in 2015: a "nothingburger." So far, he and I seem to connect far better in writing than we do in person.

COLLEGE STATION, 2019

Tonight, I am sitting in our house in Texas watching (again) some of Gleason's many videos on YouTube. In the Adam Papagan interview with Gleason in his online program, *The ASMR Talk Show* (March 25, 2019), Gleason alludes to his own mortality twice, both times related to his ongoing heart problems. In this interview, it is plainly evident that Gleason has forsaken his droll shtick which made him regionally famous in L.A. He has shed the mask of the angry, punk writer, straining to be more clever than "the man." Now that he has become part of the L.A. art establishment because of his journalistic credentials, he remarks that he doesn't want to "bite the hand that feeds you too often." This feels like Spicoli has been hired on as a teacher back at Ridgemont High.

As I watch Gleason's interview, I can see that he has significantly mellowed in recent years. Contrasted to an earlier Papagan *ASMR Talk Show* interview, these days Gleason seems to be more comfortable in his own skin. This might be attributable to his prolonged studio experience on the TV series *Skin Wars: Fresh Paint* (in 2016). His diction has also improved. For instance, he uses fewer expletives; in their place, he employs a more refined and nuanced vocabulary. He also lets the little things slide. In the newer video, Papagon adroitly points out that Gleason has become part of the art establishment, and that his identity has expanded. His growth came by ceasing to milk his identity just because it was the easy thing to do. Many artists fall into this trap of milking their gender identities, their sexual identities, their racial identities, or in Gleason's case, his punk-rock-writer identity.

On a side note, this is why I admire the artist Mark Bradford's work. He does not mine only one single theme. First, his work *is* rooted in his identity as a black man, and how he navigated two radically different worlds where he grew up: Santa Monica and South Los Angeles. But he is not solely an introspective artist. He is outward-focused as well. For example, Mark unpacks how his identity fits into American history on a macro-scale. Some of his work, like *Through Darkest America by Truck and Tank,* relates to Eisenhower's Interstate

Highway System, in which many minority communities were torn apart by the new roads. In other works, such as *Dead Hummingbird*, he highlights his impression as a young, gay, black man during the AIDS epidemic, in which so many of his friends of all races died. In one piece, *Finding Barry*, Mark specifically focuses on the marginalization of those afflicted with AIDS. Mark's identity *informs* his art; in fact, he builds bridges with his art which allow everyone to join him on his art path. Mark also explored other areas when he represented the United States at the 2017 Venice Art Biennale in his narrative *Tomorrow is Another Day,* in which he focused on the themes of marginalization, abuse of women, and women's depiction in society. But I digress...

Now, back to Gleason. In 2019, I wrote a book review on Amazon for Gleason's book, *The Century Hit Puberty: Some Essays 2010-2014*. It follows here:

> Mat Gleason's *The Century Hit Puberty: Some Essays 2010-2014* is a fantastic read, most of it. If it were a meal, it would be like the best steak ever, accompanied with overcooked mashed potatoes and mushy green beans. His book arrived in my mailbox via Amazon yesterday, and I read it in one sitting, except for a few boring chapters about music. If Gleason were curating his chapters, he might have omitted the ones about Lou Reed, the Replacements, and Leonard Cohen.
>
> If you're an artist and you cannot make it to one of Gleason's annual L.A. art boot camps, his book would be a good substitute as a primer for thriving in the SoCal art world. Much of the first half reads like a manual from a coach to his most valued player. It flows with personal, comedic, and warm tones - but it is caustic in parts, with one's best

interests in mind. For instance, Gleason admonishes the reader to delete their birth year from their website so as to not scare away youth-obsessed collectors.

Gleason's author's voice entertains because he does not limit himself to a single groove. Through the years represented in his collection of essays, one can detect him experimenting with assorted writing styles - some personal, and others rigorous... and a few are even downright Trump-like in his pithy attacks on vulnerable, overly-exposed art world figures. In the first half of his volume, he hits the ball way out the park.

In Gleason's second half though, he only bats . 500, especially in the section entitled "410 Boyd-The curse of Cocola" [on p. 152], which in my first pass was unreadable.

The top paragraph on page 27 contains some excellent art exposition: "Europeans actually get Los Angeles. New Yorkers are just embarrassed to be here and try to network during most of their stay to pad their job history for the inevitable move back to Queens. This expansive survey of postwar Los Angeles contemporary art is the brainchild of tired New York academics. In sports, they call this East Coast Bias. The history of the Los Angeles art scene is getting the 'gee whiz' media glance that Joe Torre got when he left managing the Yankees for the Dodgers. The clucking of the blizzard and brownstone crowd goes something like this: We just can't believe that everything does not happen in New York, but if you are going to commit suicide (the term New Yorkers use for leaving New York) you may as well enjoy exile in nice weather."

Gleason's use of wit and sarcasm in his excerpt (above) treads a fine line, and he pulls it off. Many lesser writers might try to be clever and unfortunately come across as snarky or small. But like an old preacher employing his best sermon illustration, Gleason returns home to his main idea, and he doesn't get lost on any rabbit trails. He occasionally throws in a dose of humility which may be rooted in his ongoing health struggles. This is endearing and makes his body-slams feel more palatable.

Speaking of "body-slams," Gleason's first section, "You Genius You," knocks the artist/reader back on their duff. Unlike the Reverend Jesse Jackson, who steadily reiterates to his audiences that "You are somebody," Gleason posits, "Well, maybe you're not somebody. Maybe your art really sucks."

It is obvious that Gleason does not think that Jerry Saltz sucks. In fact, perhaps unintentionally, as Gleason writes glowingly of Saltz, Saltz becomes the Yoda to his Skywalker; but in this case, the apprentice has become the master, especially in SoCal regional terms. Gleason is like the smallest soldier in his platoon — he can wriggle within small spaces into which Saltz cannot fit. Gleason's lifetime of experiences in and around the SoCal art world informs his insider's guide to fishing — he knows where all of the best spots are.

Some of Gleason's shining moments include his short bios of Dennis Hopper, Jackson Pollack, and Lucian Freud. The very best chapter, entitled "A Convergence of Four Art Critics," reads like a lovers' quarrel between three critics on Lumonol (Saltz, Gleason, and Robert Hughes), and one much lesser critic/troglodyte. If for no other reason, this chapter alone is worth the full price of admission.

When contrasted with his less compelling chapter on Diebenkorn's art, it makes one wonder if Gleason might be better served to write about art figures, rather than the actual works themselves. Gleason's insertion of his own person into the narrative in the "Convergence" section slyly compels the reader to root for him (the gritty L.A. City College educated scribe) as he whomps against the quintessential stuffy Yale Art school professor. It feels like Rocky I — but instead of bobbing and weaving in a boxing ring, Gleason spars alone at his keyboard in his Huntington Park home. His wife, Leigh, calls out from her office down the hall, "Mat, I see some typos!"

Shortly thereafter, Gleason and Salgado each write me a brief note of thanks. That same week, the artist Bradford Salamon writes me about the review as well: "You're a talented writer, John. Insightful review indeed. Mat has had a unique career. I didn't know [that] you are a writer."

Following this, I contact Gleason, asking if I might write an article to be included in his online art magazine. He inquires about my topic, and I share that I want to write about my interactions with many prominent L.A. art figures and their advice to me. He replies, "In my opinion, you should air it out, and do a self-published book. I think you are onto something. Write 30,000 words and self-publish on Amazon. You can sell these for $7 each. They will basically be expensive business cards. Since you will enjoy publisher's price, you can buy copies for yourself for $2 or $3; and then everyone is impressed that you have a book, and you put it in everyone's hands that you can."

His advice is illustrative of the fact that the Internet can act as a powerful leveler; it allows me access to a substantial portion of the art world. For example, I am able to write Jerry Saltz for advice regarding his writing process. He and his wife Roberta Smith are the two most revered art critics in America. Saltz advises me, "I write and rewrite and rewrite and rewrite and so on. There is NO SUCH thing as writing. There is ONLY rewriting. Go for it."

Mat Gleason adds, "Write as much as you can, every detail, go on tangents, digress, make points along the way but fill us in on every nuance... I think you are on to something." Cool. He thinks I am on to something.

The photo (below left) shows Gleason guiding Julie and I on a private tour of three L.A. museums in the summer of 2019, arranged through Airbnb. The other image (below right) is a painting I did of the artist and professor Paul Paiement, a friend of Mat Gleason. After I completed this painting, Paul invited me to a future visit at his studio!

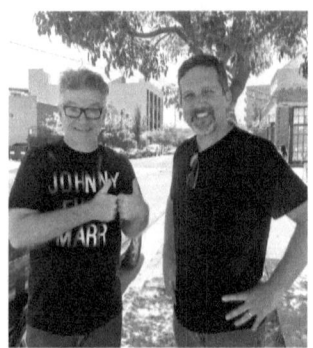
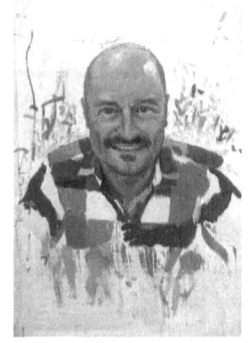

CHAPTER 21 - CONCLUSION

~

After visiting many prominent SoCal art figures, I am struck by the ubiquity of their overwhelming hospitality. But there have been a few people with closed doors along the way. There are still many other great So Cal artists with whom I would like to meet, including, Don Bachardy, Bill Wray, Lili Bernard, Faith Taylor, David Hockney, and (most importantly) Llyn Foulkes. Through it all, I have learned to enjoy the process, the act of making my art, and not to focus on success in terms of money or fame. From Llyn Foulkes' example, I now realize that it is OK to be different, and that I need not continually compare myself with other artists. You may have surmised by now that this book not only recounts my efforts to return to L.A. - it is part of the effort. If one's art is strong, and one has some pluck, then the L.A. art scene can open up its doors wider than you'd think. With a little luck, you can end up breaking bread and drinking wine with some pretty amazing people, and you may even discover some members of your tribe along the way!

ABOUT THE AUTHOR

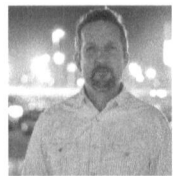

JOHN MARCELLA GRANT is an artist who focuses on figurative realism in his paintings, drawings, and sculptures. His work is in private collections in California, Texas, Europe, and Asia. Grant has a BA from UCSB, a teaching credential from UCLA, and a Masters of Architecture from Texas A&M. He is married to Julie Grant, and divides his time between College Station, TX and Seal Beach, CA. This is his first book.

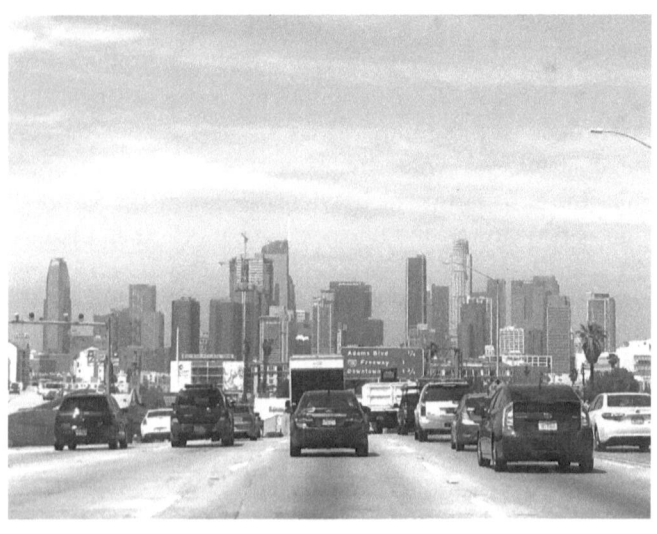

BLURBS:

"In his book *Discovering the L.A. Art World*, John Marcella Grant demonstrates the power of a simple knock on a studio door. That knock, along with the phrase 'You are my favorite artist, and we came from Texas to see you,' gained him admittance to Mark Bradford's studio in 2012, opening the door—literally and metaphorically— to the direct experience of a varied and vital group of artists and art world figures. Yes, there are some closed doors (Mark Grotjahn and Kehinde Wiley), but also real, ongoing engagements and conversations—particularly with critic/gallerist Mat Gleason and artist Bradford J. Salamon, that reward Grant's earnest approach. Told in a slightly awestruck voice and tempered with fair-mindedness, the anecdotes presented in *Discovering the L.A. Art World* provide private glimpses of a world that other less courageous writers could have never entered."
— **John Seed, Author of *My Art World***

"John Marcella Grant has an appetite for making art and experiencing it that seems insatiable. What I most like about his work is that it is honest. Words like 'honest' and 'sincere' are often used to describe an artist's work, but in this case, they are well deserved. Grant's writing seems to have this same kind of direct quality and intent. Grant has extraordinary observational skills which he puts on full display in all the work that he does." — **Bradford J. Salamon, artist**

"I don't know if I'm a guy who should be writing a blurb for John Marcella Grant, because I honestly didn't know diddle about the machinations of the L.A. fine art scene when he sent me his manuscript. However, his journey is odd and quirky and often funny; and I thought as I read through the chapters that it's better than watching a documentary. No one is playing to a camera in his book. It's just him, and sometimes his wife (and kids) and other artists. I wondered while reading it if there is a comedic script hiding somewhere inside these chapters. His book is more than about art, of course, it's about perseverance and self-doubt and fitting in and finding your tribe. — **Steve Boman, Author of** *Film School*

"This is a fun read. John Marcella Grant, like many architecture students, has had an ongoing interest in art and artists. He has pursued his interest in novel ways and has built his own successful career as an artist with understanding that comes from these encounters." — **D. Kirk Hamilton, FAIA, FACHA, EDAC, Professor, Department of Architecture at Texas A&M**

"I enjoyed John Marcella Grant's transparency as he ushers us into the world of art. The wisdom gleaned first-hand would benefit any person. Grant's initiative and desire to learn from the best is inspiring!" — **Aaron Brown, author of** *The Oracle*

"I love the concept of this book and John's writing skills make it hard to put down. I hope he turns it into a series." — **Kent Twitchell, artist**

"Frightening and Riveting" — **Laddie John Dill, Artist**